Flashes *of* Life

True Tales of the Extraordinary Ordinary

Pamela S. Wight

Flashes *of* Life
True Tales of the Extraordinary Ordinary

Pamela S. Wight

ISBN 978-17345730-5-3

BORGO
PUBLISHING

www.borgopublishing.com

Printed in the USA

TABLE OF CONTENTS

Introduction *1*

Section I
Looking in
the Mirror

Who Am I? 3
Straight Hair...5
Dancing Our Age? 8
What's in the Middle of Your Middle Name?...................9
Good Morning, Moonshine 12
Breakfast of Champions 14
Fluffing My Aura 16

Section II
Fun Family Drama

How to Embarrass Your Kids.......................................19
A Renewal 21
Love's Labor Lost?...24
Mother-in-Law 26
Lost and Found...28
Grilled Cheese 30
It's All Golden 33
Nap Time..35
Joy 37
What Is It About Women and Their Feet? 38

Section III
Life Is Funny

Burnt Toast...41
Adventures in Babysitting..43
Contracts, Audrey Hepburn, and Miracles 46
Whistle While You Work..48
Fear of (Not) Flying..50
Under the Princess Canopy 52
No RE-lax at LAX 54
Scammed! 56

Section IV	My Dog Is a Zen Master	59
For the Dogs	Searching for Your "People"	60
	Sharing the Divine	62
	Oxen Mystic	64
	Walking the Human	66
	Early Morning Spirits	68
Section V	Open-Mouthed Kisses	71
The Extraordinary	Buttercups, Bollywood, and World Peace	73
Ordinary	Loving Shrimp	75
	Firm Support	77
	Eating the Broccoli	79
	Calm DOWN!	81
	The Weight of the Soul	83
	A Solitary Surprise	85
Section VI	Spa Stress	89
Time Off	Family Reunion	92
	Ocean People	95
	How Was Your Vacation, Erma?	98
	A Whale of a Good Time	101
	Tunnel Vision	103
Section VII	A Perfectly Imperfect Love	107
Relationships	Love Letters	110
	Benji	112
	Yesterday	114
	The Nest, Emptied	117
	The Bed Post	119
	What's in a Name?	120
	Pot Pie	123
Section VIII	Silly Love Songs	125
Musing	Letter to Myself, 1969	126
	The Long and Winding Road	128
	Looking in the Mirror	131
Acknowledgements		*132*
About the Author		*133*

*My short stories are like soft shadows I have set out in the world,
faint footprints I have left. I remember exactly where I set down each
and every one of them, and how I felt when I did.
Short stories are like guideposts to my heart....*

—HARUKI MURAKAMI

Introduction

My "FLASH MEMOIR" INCLUDES LIGHT-HEARTED SHORT STORIES ABOUT MY LIFE. I hope these flash narratives remind you of similar experiences in your life. Collectively, we nod our heads, chuckle, acknowledge how much we have in common. I believe that we all share "aha" sparks that occur in our everyday, ordinary lives. My family is your family. My loves are your loves. My smiles are your smiles.

Many of my "soft shadowed" stories have been posted in my blog, *www.roughwighting.net*. I was hesitant about starting a blog (a website that's written in an informal style for business or personal use), but when my nephew learned that I was soon to publish my first book, he insisted that I needed one for promotion. I began to write weekly "vignettes" about an ordinary life that everyone could relate to, because when we pay attention, we realize our lives are quite extraordinary.

I charged headlong, counting only two blog followers: Nephew Chris and me. Within a year, the amount increased to over a hundred. Seven years later, a few days after my mom died at the age of 96, the number of my blog followers popped up on my screen—4,444—my mom's favorite number.

My mother sparkles throughout some of these pages, as do family members and friends and dogs. After all, each of them is a guidepost in my life.

My wish is that as you read my stories, you'll find your guideposts too.

ONE

Looking in the Mirror

Who Am I?

I'M A CURLY-HAIRED WOMAN WHO LOVES FAIRYTALE FANTASY, LONG WALKS along the water, communing silently with babies and animals, and reading for hours in a deep plush chair while sipping Tropical Green tea.

I dislike vapid, vain chatter; inconsiderate drivers who turn without signaling; wayward souls who act as if they run the world; grocery carts with broken wheels; men who pinch women's rears (yes, still!); unanswered e-mails; unplucked eyebrows; arguments; orange vests; and fruit drinks.

My heart soars with the soft, whisper-filled kisses of little ones; a sun salutation on a Hawaiian beach; a spontaneous loud laugh from a colleague; a handful of M&M's, particularly the green or blue ones; a sudden embrace from my irreplaceable guy.

The sounds I most enjoy: the swish of pens on paper (and the clacking of laptop keys) during one of my creative writing classes; the pounding surf on the New Jersey seashore; the beat of a Beatles tune; the bark of Henry, the dog, as he sits in front of his cookie jar; the beginning melody of The Nutcracker Suite ballet; the soft plop of an omelet-filled plate placed in front of me at a sunny San Francisco corner café; the "hello Pammy" call from my effervescent, magnetic mom.

Life is worthwhile because of soft classical music on a cold Sunday morning; two-hour conversations with a long-time friend; a tall, diffident son who stares deeply into my eyes and says, "Love you, Mom"; a two-year-old grandchild who sits quietly, attentively on my lap while listening to *Good Night Moon*; writing stories on a foggy afternoon about people I've never met; a man who runs out to buy my special Earl Gray tea latte, non-fat milk with foam at 6:15 in the morning; a beautiful daughter who wears her heart on every sleeve and her love in her morning glory eyes.

That's who I am.

Who are you?

Straight Hair

AT FOURTEEN YEARS OF AGE, I WANT TO LOOK LIKE JANE ASHER.

You know, Jane, Paul McCartney's girlfriend. Jane of the tiny frame, adorable smile, and long straight hair. Hair as straight as grass.

I have curly, wavy, crazy hair.

But I want Paul. The "cute" Beatle—the one who I know is my soul mate. If we ever get to meet, he'll look at me longingly (if I have straight hair) and leave Jane and we'll be together, forever.

I walk to the drugstore with my friend Judy, where I use my babysitting money for the product I've lusted over for months: Curl Free. Judy just rolls her eyes when I buy the box and we race home to my bathroom.

My mom is out, probably playing bridge, so I keep the bathroom door open to dispel some of the smell that is so putrid, we both gag. Once I combine one bottle in the box with another smaller bottle hidden in the bottom, we race out of the room. The upstairs now smells like rotten eggs, my brother's farts, and sauerkraut, all rolled into one malodorous bouquet.

"You aren't really putting that on your hair!" Judy exclaims as we inhale huge breaths of fresh air on my back porch.

"For forty-five minutes," I reply.

"I can't take that smell. I'd better go home." Judy leaves, and by doing so, I wash my hands of her companionship forever. Our friendship is finished with one long whiff of Curl Free.

But I still have work to do. My mom is reaching for the front door, holding two bags of groceries. Oh, no!

I race to the bathroom and shut and lock the door. The smell has only gotten stronger, but I clench my jaw and use the comb provided in the box to rake the goo throughout my hair. The solution is white and putrid, and within minutes stings so badly I think my scalp is on fire.

I sprint to the sink and turn on the cold water, ready to wash the glop out immediately.

But then I think of Jane.

Turning off the water, I blindly open the bottom drawer underneath the sink and feel for my hidden Beatle magazine, the one with a photo of Jane and Paul attending a play in London. However, my eyes are watering so badly, I can't see the picture.

"OW-OW-OW-OW!" I scream.

"Pammy, are you all right in there?"

Oh, shoot. I forgot about my mom. "I'm fine, Mom."

"Are you sure? Something smells funny. Are you feeling okay?"

Face flaming red from embarrassment, and probably from the beginning of second degree burns, I shout out, "I'm FINE."

And then I throw my head into the bottom of the sink and turn on the water, emitting groans as the cold water soothes the burning sensation. I only lasted ten minutes with Curl Free. Will it make a difference?

I towel off my hair, now as stiff as dry wheat, open the bathroom door and suffer through my mother's questions about my intestinal problems. "Do you have a stomach ache?" she asks worriedly.

"No, Mom," I respond, biting the inside of my lip. My hair is drying rapidly this warm May day, and I do not look like Jane Asher.

I dash past my mother and head to the basement. I hate the basement, so she is suspicious. "What are you doing now?"

"Ironing," I answer.

Supposedly, that's the next best thing for hair straightening.

Dancing Our Age?

THE SONG COMES ON THE RADIO AND I FEEL A HIP TWITCH. I RUN FROM THE home office to the living room to be closer to the music, and the other hip twitches. My right foot hits the Oriental carpet with a stomp and then both feet hit the carpet hard—toe foot, toe foot. My heart lifts with the beat, and I scoot to the stereo and turn up the volume.

Rock and roll, baby.

Suddenly, I'm twenty again. College dances. I close my eyes and smell the spilled beer, the sweaty college boys, the perfumed girls. Ode to Joy. Old Spice. I see us, moving our hips back and forth, jumping up and down to the beat.

Laughing. Shouting. Wild and Free.

I open my eyes, dancing with a huge grin on my face. The dog hops up from his place in the sun to see what his crazy mistress is doing. He looks astonished, then runs over to me, jumping up as if he, too, wants to dance.

Then I glance toward the far wall. The mirror shows the scene. A middle-aged woman with doggy, dancing in the middle of living room on a Wednesday afternoon. The college scene fades, my smile disappears. Where's the cute twenty-year-old? Who the hell is this freaky lady?

I turn my back on the mirror, order the dog to "Sit!" and "Stay!" and I dance like crazy until the song ends.

What's in the Middle of Your Middle Name?

MANY MIDDLE NAMES ARRIVE IN THE MIDDLE OF CONFUSION, COMPROMISE, AND even confrontation.

Take my middle name.

Well, for the first thirty years of my life, you couldn't have taken it, because I didn't have one.

When I became sentient enough, around the age of six, I realized that, unlike my friends (Beverly Lynn Landing, Julie Glory Wyckoff, Barbara Ann Bancroft), I had no three-word title to deliver on the right-hand side of my school papers.

Just plain Pamela Wight.

When I was seven, I asked my parents what my middle name was. They did that "parent look" over my head, the look that said, "Don't say anything," while replying, "You don't have one."

When I was nine I asked my parents why I didn't have a middle name. They did that parent look again, but this time I stomped my foot and demanded an answer.

My mom explained, "When you were born, your dad and I couldn't agree on what your middle name should be."

Dad added, with love in his eyes, "So we agreed to give you NO middle name."

Boy, that made me mad. *So glad the argument turned out well for them,* I thought, *but what about me?* I explained these feelings to them, as only a nine-year-old can, something like, "BUT I WANT A MIDDLE NAME NOOOOWWWW."

So they calmed me with compromise.

"Pammy," my dad said earnestly, "when you're old enough, you can decide your own middle name."

Wow, that stopped my protest immediately. Really? My middle name could be anything?

My mom, seeing how much pleasure this idea gave me, said over my head and into my father's ear, "Let's see what she wants it to be right now. Why wait?"

So they asked me what I'd choose for my middle name. I thought, and thought, and thought carefully for over a week.

Then I came back to them and announced that my name was now Pamela Thankful Wight.

Uh-oh. That parental look across my head occurred again. After much "discussion" (me crying and them pleading), we came to a compromise. When I turned fifteen, I could create a middle name for myself, no matter what it was, and that would be that.

Well, six years later, I approached my parents on my birthday and said, "Okay, I'm ready."

They didn't know what I was talking about! They had forgotten about my middle name.

I certainly had not.

I chose the perfect name. I heard it sung, over and over again, by the Beatles. The girl they sang about was beautiful and romantic and desired.

That would be me.

"My middle name," I declared, "is Michelle."

Well, you'd think I'd said, "Ungrateful," or "Freaky," or "Drugs and Alcohol," because my parents hated the name "Michelle."

"You only like it because of the Beatles. Wait a few more years, then decide," my dad said.

"I will never NOT like the name Michelle. Pamela Michelle Wight. It's perfect!" I argued over and over, but to no avail.

So for the next fifteen years, I had no middle name. Not for all my college applications, or employment applications, or even on my first mortgage statement.

I was Pamela "Nameless" Wight.

Until I met my guy who became forever mine.

And guess one of the first things he did after he declared undying love for me?

He gave me a middle initial.

He began calling me Pamela S. Wight.

As soon as we began to co-exist (and then legally marry), he filled out our rental apps, taxes, insurance forms, school release forms for our kids, etc., etc., with his name and mine: Pamela S. Wight.

Only one slight problem.

To this day, he has still never told me what the "S" stands for.

Good Morning, Moonshine

I OPEN ONE EYE AND READ THE YELLOW-TINTED CLOCK—THE ONE I'VE WANTED to move away from my night table for years, but never do.

1:45 a.m.

I sigh and open the other eye. Really? Because right now my sight is rather blurry. Maybe the clock says 9:05. Ah, that would be bliss, to have slept through the night, an unlikely occurrence for most women over the age of, well, over that age.

When I think about it (and really, I might as well think now, because it's unlikely I'll get back to sleep), we women have gotten a bum rap. Finally, when we're over that certain age—too old to have babies screaming for a bottle or teenagers breaking a midnight curfew—so we can finally sleep undisturbed, our bodies won't let us.

Just another example of why God must not be a woman.

I laugh at my idiotic mutterings. However, as I listen to my husband snore softly next to me, having absolutely no problem with sleep, I wonder if I'm not so crazy after all.

I stare out the window and close my eyes. 100, 99, 98, 97....

"Cheep! Cheep, cheep!"

My eyes snap open. Birds? At a quarter to two in the morning?

"Tweet, cheep, chirp, chirp, chirp!"

An entire melody. Impossible. Isn't it? I always thought that birds woke up with the sun. So what's the singing about?

I rise from the bed as husband rolls over, comfortable as a dog; in fact, I almost stumble over our golden, who is flat on his back on the floor by my side of the bed, legs open wide, eyes closed, mouth in a wide grin. *Men! They are blessed*, I mumble.

But then I realize that it's light enough so that I can see the dog's happy torpor. Maybe the clock is broken, and I've slept six full hours to wake with the rising sun. Yippee! I race to the window and gape.

A spectacularly bright full moon gleams back at me, as pleased as the slumbering dog. Huh, so the moon is male too! And the moon is so bright, the birds got confused and woke up and began to sing their version of "Good Morning Starshine, the Earth says hello!" song. (*Good Morning Starshine* by Oliver)

I stumble toward the kitchen and the oven clock. 2:03. Drat.

I pause, wondering what to do now. Warm up some milk? Munch on a cookie? I open up the cookie tin and pick up a chocolate chip bar made earlier in the day. As I stand on one leg, then the other (working on my yoga balance), I stare at the refrigerator door, full of family pictures made into magnets. Our kids, grandkids, friends, all smiling out at me. Thank goodness we never bought one of those "new" silver steel fridges. If we'd gone modern, we'd never be able to slap our life onto the front of it.

I bite into another chunk of the sweet gooey bar as I peruse the photo of our sweet grandson. There's a picture of him as an infant. Just a few days ago I'd spent a couple of hours playing with the one-year-old. As I left to return home, the toddler wrapped his arms around my neck and opened his mouth wide, like a fish, and pressed it against my mouth—his kiss goodbye. God, I'd melted like ice on hot tar.

Now I tiptoe back to the moon-infused bedroom, dog unmoved, husband still in dreamland, bed inviting me to join them in mindless slumber.

What the heck, I'll try.

Breakfast of Champions

I USED TO FIX MYSELF A BOWL OF CEREAL EVERY MORNING.

I hate cereal.

I hated it as a child; I hated it when I fixed it for years as an adult; and I hate it now, whether Cheerios, or Shredded Wheat, or Raisin Bran.

My mom is the reason I hate cereal (she's smiling and protesting at the same time as she reads this, I bet.) But really, that's what our "big fights" were about when I was a teenager.

"Pammy, you can't go to school without breakfast."

"I hate Wheaties," I'd moan.

"Wheaties are good for you. Look at your brother—he's on his third bowl."

"Well, he's a champion. I'm not," I'd retort. Sarcastic for a fifteen-year-old, but my brother was a successful swimmer—trophies all over the house—so a bit of sisterly bile sprang out sometimes.

Maybe he's the reason I hate cereal!

No matter, at sixteen I discovered chocolate Instant Breakfast. I'd drink it at 7:30 a.m. in front of my mom's scowling face. She'd explain to my dad, "At least she's not going to school on an empty stomach."

And then, fast forward to years later.

I found myself making my children eat cereal before school. The difference was that they liked it. I still didn't, but I felt like I had to be a good role model, so I'd scarf down a small bowl while my son and daughter cheerfully compared Cheerio holes every gosh-darn morning.

Until suddenly, a year ago, I stopped pouring milk into my Shredded Wheat bowl mid-stream and said out loud, "Why the hell are you doing this?!" I threw out the cereal and milk and the next day bought a fresh loaf of wheat bread.

Now my routine is a slice of toast with a dollop of peanut butter and strawberry jam on top.

I'm sure there's a bigger message in here somewhere, like:

- we adults get so stuck in our routines, we need to stop and think about what we really want. Or,
- life is short, give up what is unnecessary. Or,
- live life to the fullest—enjoy every minute, and every morsel.

But really, all I'm saying is that I'm so much happier with my mornings.

Fluffing My Aura

JUNE IS A HAPPY MONTH FOR MY FAMILY. BUT IT'S ALSO A MONTH WHEN I NEED to fluff my aura a lot.

Until a few months ago, I never knew about the joy of fluffing. Sure, I'm a yoga-believer. I try to meditate once in a while and, during my long walks, I definitely find myself in a "different mindspace" at times.

But normally, I'm as stressed as the next person. Life, you know? It springs surprises and quirks, leaps and jerks, every day. Sometimes, I just want to hide under a good book and escape—but most times I'm unable to get away from the hustle and bustle of daily irritations, situations, and difficult deliberations.

But in the middle of the warrior pose during one of my get-away-from-the-grind (for sixty minutes) yoga classes, a new instructor began fluttering her arms from her chest to above her head, as if she were a ballet dancer in the middle of performing Swan Lake. She seemed to be fluffing invisible "wings" up and about.

We five yogic warriors ended our pose, staring at her without comprehension. Our expressions were quite readable (i.e., "What the hell is she doing?")

The tall, reed-thin, attractive woman laughed lightly and said, "It's been one of those days. I'm sorry, I need to get rid of the bad vibes. Start anew. You know—fluff my aura."

Well, we didn't know, but the more she talked about it (and fluffed) the more we all became converts, and by the end of the class, we were fluffing our auras, dispensing with the dark and inviting in the light and the bright.

You may laugh at me, but I felt a great deal better when I returned to the rest of my day.

So now it's June, when I celebrate so many birthdays that my aura begins to collapse. My son was born on June 4, my daughter on June 10. Our special angel dog, Henry, was a June 15 puppy, and two of my grandsons move up an age on June 15 and June 27. Oh, and then my guy and I commemorate our anniversary on June 30.

Why, you ask, is fluffing needed?

LIFE SWINGS BY TOO FAST! It was only yesterday that I felt my first child lifted out of my womb (thanks to a fast-thinking surgeon) perfectly formed and flawless, lying in my arms within seconds and melding my soul into hers for all time.

She turns forty-two in June.

My aura dims.

For thirteen years the family celebrated Henry's birth with an extra rump rub, a small tub of doggie ice cream, and a long walk where he was allowed to sniff for as long as he wanted.

We miss him, gone now for several years, although his favorite toy is discovered mysteriously in different corners of the house every so often. I believe he is fluffing our aura.

Birthdays and anniversaries are joyous occasions, but they also make us stop and think about the past, the present, and the future. We begin to stress: Did I do enough in the past? Am I doing the best I can in the present? How much future do I have?

That's when I need to start fluffing my aura.

Will you join me? The more we fluff, the stronger the light.

TWO

Fun Family Drama

How to Embarrass Your Kids

YES, I SEE THE QUICK SMIRK ON YOUR FACE. I HEAR YOU THINKING ABOUT THE time you sang, "I Can't Get No … Satisfaction," loudly while standing in line at the grocery store as your kids squirmed in … dissatisfaction.

It's not like we start out trying to mortify our kids. They initiate it!

For instance, my guy has worn long tennis socks with his shorts since he was a studly twenty-five-year-old, and by god, he's sticking with those socks (or ones like them) for his entire life. So, when our kids were … kids … they moaned on vacations as we walked the beach together in July, or attended swimming lessons or tennis lessons, or even soccer games, and they had to endure their dad in shorts and "tall" socks.

They'd save their allowance and buy short, thick Agassi tennis socks and stick them in their dad's sock drawer (and throw out the offending "tall" socks, of course). But by that time, tall socks had become a symbol of our independence, our stubbornness, and our parenting. *No child of ours was going to tell us what we could or could not wear, or sing, or even admire.*

One day I was driving my kids home from a lesson—ballet or soccer or piano or chess or, well, the list goes on. Because we lived off a scenic, hilly road called "Paradise Drive," we always passed many buff bicyclists. On this particular sunny afternoon, I unknowingly let out a sigh while exclaiming, "Look at the calves on that man."

My son and daughter both bellowed, in two long syllables: "MOOOOOMMMMM!"

"What?" I asked innocently.

"You're married," my son expounded. "You can't look at another man's legs!"

I came close to muttering back, "I'm married, but I'm not dead," but instead said, "I'm just commenting on the muscles this guy has built by bicycling so hard."

No good. My kids were adamant that I should not and could not notice the muscles on any man but their dad.

I realized then that I'd just found a supreme opportunity for future parental embarrassment. So each time the kids and I drove home on Paradise Drive and we passed a well-muscled bicyclist, I'd open my mouth and begin, "Wow, look at the...." And they'd stop me with groans of dismay and the two-syllable pronunciation of my name. If one of their friends was in the car with us, my children would blush stop-sign red before I even pointed.

Aah, the perks of being a parent.

P.S. I won't even start with how my stories embarrass my (now adult) children. Let's just say, I'm not supposed to write about negligées, sexual attraction, bedroom eyes, or passion (if you've read my books *Twin Desires* and *The Right Wrong Man*, you know I still embarrass my kids horribly).

A Renewal

BACK WHEN I WAS LIVING IN NEW ENGLAND AND MY BOY WAS A SENIOR IN college, he and I decided to go on a road trip. I had high hopes of mother/son time, but the drive began in silence.

As I maneuvered in the harsh steady rain, my twenty-one-year-old breathed slowly and steadily, sound asleep as the car whipped through the Connecticut highway puddles. We were on our way to Delaware, a seven-hour drive in good weather, to visit my father, Sean's grandfather. I had been amazed when Sean offered to lose a weekend at college, one of the last few remaining ones before he graduated in a month.

When I picked him up from his Boston campus at 10:00 a.m., the rain began to plop, plop, plop. Sean had always been a sucker for the rhythmic motion of a rainstorm. It put him to sleep when he was a child, and here he was, no longer a boy, sandpaper fuzz on his face because he'd been up all night finishing a paper, head tilted sideways in a posture of child-like vulnerability, mouth open, eyes closed in dreams I'd never know.

Every week I'd call Sean when he was in school, conversation difficult because the background noise was always deafening. I could just see those randy young men skidding down the fraternity house hallways like half-grown pups, drinking, laughing, shouting at the top of their lungs just because they could. Sean must do that, too, but at home he was always just quiet. When he offered to drive with me to Pop Pop's, my first thought was, "Aha! I'll have him all to myself. Now he'll talk!" But instead, he was snoring, and I was holding myself as stiff as a board, hovering over the steering wheel like an old woman protecting a treasure, trying to see at least four feet in front of me as we raced 60 miles per hour in the messy storm.

An hour later, the rain lightened up and, as if on signal, Sean yawned and stretched and looked out the window. "Oh, this isn't too bad," he said, and I would have strangled him except my hands were clenched on either side of the wheel.

"Hmm," I muttered.

"What have we got here?" Sean asked as he turned to the back seat and inspected the cooler I had wisely brought along. Not only had I stocked it with casseroles and a cake for my dad, but also sandwiches and drinks for our lunch on the drive down. "Wow, Mom, you're awesome," he said as he brought out a ham and Swiss cheese sub and two Diet Cokes.

"Hmm," I replied a little more lightheartedly. I surfed through the radio stations, trying to find some music that we both would like.

"Wait, I have a better idea," he said, and he reached into his backpack and pulled out his portable CD collection. Oh no, I moaned to myself. With my luck, it would be rap or some avant-garde music that I'd absolutely hate. I never could determine Sean's music taste. One minute he listened to Beethoven, the next minute to Eminem.

The music began. Classic Beatles – the HELP CD. I looked at him sharply. "You don't have to…."

"I love this CD, Mom," he said. We both began singing the words out loud and out of tune: "I've just seen a face I can't forget the name or place…."

"You listen to this at college?" I asked as we laughed with the last note.

"All the time," he said. "You got me to appreciate good music. Growing up, thanks to you, I never heard anything but the Beatles and classic 60s rock and roll. It's the best."

I nodded my head in agreement.

"You okay, Mom? Want me to drive a little?"

"No, I'm fine. Just a little worried about Pop Pop."

"Yeah, that's why I wanted to come. I don't get to see him that much. We'll just hang out with him, play checkers, take him to the grocery store, play more checkers, watch him smoke…."

"You okay with that?"

"Yeah, and it will help you out. I didn't want you driving down here by yourself. And it gives us time to talk. We never have time to just talk, you know? I'm too busy with school, you're busy with your work and writing and stuff. I'm worried. What if I don't find a job? What if I have to come home? I'll die…."

We both chuckled.

"And after four years at an expensive college, what if I end up being a waiter?" he continued. "I'm worried. And I'm not dating anyone because I don't know where I'll be and it's stupid to get interested in someone when who knows what the next year will bring. You know? Why didn't I listen to you guys and go for an engineering degree? I don't know, I wish you'd made me…."

He went on and on. And on. I listened to the Beatles, listened to my son talk like he was eight again, and felt renewed as a mom, renewed as a friend to my growing-up son. The sun suddenly burst through the clouds, and my eyes got a little wet.

"Mom? You okay?"

"Just need my sunglasses," I lied. And then I listened some more.

Love's Labor Lost?

WHEN MY FRIENDS FIRST LEARNED I WAS GOING TO BE A "GRANDMAW," SOME OF them guffawed at me, as if my freedom, feistiness, and femaleness would soon be out the window. After all, what does a grandmother do but bake cookies, babysit, and bring out the photos of her grandbabies too often?

In protest, a month before my first grandbabe was born, I participated in a 10k run and then my guy and I flew off to Italy to share a villa with friends. No old biddy waiting for grandchildren was I!

In July my daughter went into labor, calling me at 11:04 p.m. to let me know she was on the way to the hospital. Her husband texted every hour at first with updates. My guy groaned when the phone beeped at my pillow at 1:00 a.m. and 2:00 a.m. and so forth. By 8:00 a.m. no progress, and as the sun grew high in the sky, I became a crazed, aged, terrified woman. I walked the woods around our house like a crone, startling the wild kingdom, tearing my graying hair out by the roots.

WHY WAS IT TAKING SO LONG?

I called my good friend the minister, who hadn't ministered to me in years and now lived thousands of miles away, begging him to pray for my daughter and as yet unborn grandchild. He soothed me as my feet crunched on moss and dead leaves, and assured me that all would be well.

I didn't believe him.

So, despite my daughter's wishes, I made my guy drive us to the hospital so we could pace in the waiting room. The receptionist assured me (five times) that my daughter was in the labor room. My son-in-law had last texted an hour ago that she'd been pushing for four hours. I wanted to MURDER the doctor who let her (and my grandbaby) go through this ordeal. My guy would gather me in his arms every so often and whisper "reeeelaxxxxx," but I couldn't.

Was this what being a grandmother meant? Good Lord, if I'd known, I would have handed better birth control to my children as soon as they hit reproductive age.

My cell phone bleeped—a text! Wait, it wasn't from my son-in-law. The text was from the twenty-nine-year-old son of a friend who lived across the country, who was also a friend of my daughter. The text read:

CONGRATULATIONS GRANDMA!

Wait. What?

I texted back and said, "No baby yet."

He replied via text, "Um, according to your son-in-law there is."

Wait. What?

No other message was on my cell phone. I stalked the receptionist, who suddenly was terribly busy and ignored me.

My guy told me to SIT DOWN.

Three minutes later, our son-in-law walked out to us, zombie-like, and collapsed in my arms, crying out, "Everything is perfect!"

I started crying too, of course, instantly forgiving him for sending out a group text one second after the birth, but not realizing that my cell number wasn't included.

Because at that moment, as I became a grandmother, everything was perfect.

Love's labor won.

Mother-in-Law

HE BEGGED ME TO HELP, SO I CRAWLED OUT OF MY WARM SUBURBAN BED AT 6:00 a.m. to make the forty-five-minute trip to the other side of the universe—Boston.

"The baby's sick," my son-in-law explained to me during the early morning call with a voice as desperate as a new father's can be. "Neither of us can miss another day of work, and I have an 8:00 a.m. court case. Please, Madre, can you help?"

Since the birth of my granddaughter, my name had changed from "Pam," to "Madre," and I was still coping with my new image. But I hopped into my car and joined the commuters in the bumper-to-bumper early-morning traffic.

"I am grandmother, hear me roar," I exclaimed to myself as I walked five frigid blocks from the car through the narrow city streets to the tiny townhome. My empathy and desire to help was unlimited until I knocked on the locked door three times with no response.

With frozen fingers, I pushed buttons on my cell phone and called my daughter, who was already halfway to her teaching job.

"Your husband is not answering the doorbell!" I shouted in a sweet grandmotherly voice.

"Oh," she replied, honking simultaneously at some crazy Boston driver. "He probably fell back asleep. Pound on the door, or try his cell phone."

"WHAT?" I screamed. She hung up, so I pounded, to no avail. Then I blew on my fingers so I could press the cell phone buttons to call him.

Twice.

No answer.

My Madre-ness was receding into pure unadulterated bitch. I checked my watch. 7:15. What happened to the important court case?

I hit the doorbell with my now-numb digit and didn't release. Finally, the dog barked and son-in-law opened the door, bleary-eyed and yawning, wearing beat-up shorts he had obviously just pulled on.

"Oh!" he said. The baby began to cry from her crib. "Thank God you're here!"

I smiled like a saint. I decided I'd just guaranteed no bad mother-in-law jokes from him, ever.

Lost and Found

HOW MANY ITEMS HAVE YOU LOST IN YOUR LIFETIME? TOO MANY TO COUNT ON two hands, I bet. How about in just a year? Eyeglasses, socks, mittens, scarves, yoga mats, reservations, friends (hopefully not!), shoes, books— oh dear, the list can go on and on.

But how many of you can say you lost a car?

I raise my hand.

My "mother-in-law" story describes the day I saved my son-in-law's (SIL) butt. No, not really, but I did come to his rescue, babysitting early in the morning so he could go to work. What I didn't relate was the rest of the story.

"You have to be back here by noon," I had admonished as I comforted the baby and said goodbye to SIL at 7:40 a.m. "I can't miss my 12:45 doctor's appointment."

I admit, I worried that SIL would forget. He could get lost in his job while reading reams of detailed court cases and lawsuits and … but no, he entered the door at 11:58 a.m. with a smile and a long verbal paragraph of thanks for helping him out.

I left him and my little grandbaby feeling happy, useful, relaxed, and … five blocks later, confused. Where'd I park my car? I was sure it was here, although in this part of the city, all the narrow old streets looked the same.

I walked up and down Revere Street, then Pearl, and even Brown. No car.

I returned to Revere, noting that no cars were parked on the street side where I thought I'd left mine. Suspicious, I walked ten yards to the closest sign.

"Street Cleaning
9:00 a.m. – 3:00 p.m.
3rd Thursday every month"

No.
Couldn't be.
What day was it? I checked my phone calendar as I began to race back to my daughter's townhome. Not only was it Thursday, it was the third Thursday of the month.

S H I T!

I called SIL. Before he got out a perplexed "Hi," I told him my dilemma. "Take my car!" he responded immediately. "I'll find yours!"

As I ran up their brick stairs, the front door opened and keys dangled from SIL's fingers. I grabbed them and flew to his ginormous fluorescent blue Toyota SUV.

I don't remember how I drove that truck across the Charles River and thirty miles farther, but I got to my doctor's appointment on time.

And SIL found my towed car in a nasty city lot, rescued it with a $125 ransom payment, and brought it back to me the next day.

As we exchanged cars I thought: I lost a car but I found another reason why I'm glad my daughter married this guy!

Grilled Cheese

"Sit down and don't move."

This is the first time in my life I can order my mom around, and she has to listen!

She sits on the couch, back against the long floral armrest, head against an added pillow, legs straight in front of her on the rest of the couch, more pillows raising her feet.

"But," she protests, "I know where the butter is, and the pan to grill the bread, and don't use the new tomatoes, use the ones in the vegetable bin, and I'm not sure if the cheddar cheese is on the left side of the refrigerator, or the bottom shelf, and...."

"Stop!" I command. "I can figure it out."

I'm not a kid any more. In fact, I've raised children, now adults, who thrived on my cooking, but my mom still thinks I can't make a grilled cheese sandwich without her help.

I take a deep breath and look at her sternly, but lovingly. "You need to keep your feet up right now. You've just had surgery. I have taken a five-hour train trip to stay with you and wait on you. So sit down and enjoy it!" I leave the room with a smirk on my face.

Of course, five minutes later I'm cursing under my breath. Where the hell does she store her pans? Her apartment is small, her kitchen as tiny as an elf's, and it has already taken me four minutes, thirty-eight seconds to find a spatula and a knife to cut the cheese.

No pan means no grilled cheese sandwiches, so I open more cabinets and grit my teeth.

"The bottom of the stove," Mom shouts from the living room.

I open the drawer below the oven, seemingly hidden until now, and sweetly shout out, "Got it!" *Why couldn't she have told me that in the first place?* I whistle happily as I slice and melt the butter in the pan.

"Don't use oil or that spray stuff, butter works best!" she suggests unnecessarily.

I walk briskly back into the living room. Tennis is on TV. "Thirty-love," the commentator whispers excitedly. Yup, I think, it's 30-0 right here, in this little apartment, and I'm the one not getting my serves in.

"Mom, luv," I begin.

She looks up at me innocently. I walk over and fluff up the pillows behind her, check her water class. It could use more ice. "Yes?" she asks. "Do you need any help?"

"Not at all!" I answer. I pick up her glass and announce. "You need more water. Ten glasses a day—at least!" I bounce back to the kitchen and notice that the butter is turning brown. Whoops. As I add more ice to her glass, I throw some slices of bread into the pan, race the ice water back to Mom and her tray, then race back to the kitchen. Now the bread is turning brown, and I haven't added the cheese yet.

"Damn," I shout out.

Two seconds later, I hear the clip, clip, clip of her walker, and she is standing beside me, clucking and reaching out for the cheese, the butter, the tomato. In a span of three minutes, the smells of a toasty warm grilled cheese and tomato sandwich are wafting through the small three-room apartment.

"Yum!" she says, turning off the stove top. "Sit down and I'll fix you a glass of Diet Coke. I'm starving, aren't you?"

As she arranges a dish on her walker tray and sashays back toward the couch, I admit defeat, but also realize a cheery thought.

She's healing quite well, much faster than the doctor's prediction.

It's All Golden

THE CITY SPARKLES AFTER A RAINSTORM SO, IF YOU HAVE A CHANCE, DRIVE OVER the Golden Gate Bridge, around noon, when a Pacific Ocean storm has just blown through the Gate, Marin County, and the mountains beyond with gale force winds and driving, ravenous rain.

By 9:00 a.m., after a noisy storm-riddled night, the air is clear and fresh; white and gray puffy clouds dot the sky. Some thunder tries to roll over Mt. Tam and Mt. Diablo, but then it sighs slowly, giving in to springtime optimism.

Like me, flying out of the office at noon and racing over the Golden Gate Bridge to meet my thirty-year-old son, once my "hard child," as hard as sleet on soft green grass.

I was the grass.

Sometimes he mowed me down when he was a child and teenager, with his sharp edges and relentless questions. "Why can't I play paint ball on a school day?" "Why do we have to stay home during school vacation?" "Why do I have to study when I get good grades anyway?" "Why do you always say NO?"

Soft grass was I back then, roughening to a weed-like texture with his bombardment of "whys."

So why, now, am I soaring over San Francisco Bay in anticipation of meeting that same son for lunch?

The day brightens with every mile I travel; the city looms ahead like a white Oz, all new and gleaming and magical. The streets stretch smoothly ahead of me, leading me down Lombard, up Van Ness, over Broadway, and then right onto the Embarcadero.

My son calls three times, checking on my progress, assuring himself that I'm coming, that Marin County hasn't gobbled me up in my activities of work, walking, writing—wearing out by mid-afternoon.

"No, no," I insist through my hands-free cell phone speaker. "I'm on Front Street. I'm parking; I'm walking toward you...."

There.

And my "hard" child, the one who has loved me like an old man loves his eighty-year-old wife, the son who charmed me with flowers when he was ten while I was still gritting my teeth over his demands—that son now waits for me with a trimmed beard highlighting his welcoming smile, his dimple hidden by the thick brown hair, his lips touching my cheek lightly, softly, as he whispers,

"Hi, Mom."

Nap Time

Have you noticed how the sleep of babies is so total, so full of abandon? I never tire of watching my grandbabies sleep, although it's somewhat nerve-wracking.

For instance, near nap time, little year-old Sophie roams the room like a truck driver on ten cups of coffee, then plops on the floor and exclaims, "Bitty bah dee duh rre tum tum toe!" She is quite certain that whatever she has said is philosophically salient, and I tend to agree with her.

But when it's time to put her down for her nap, she fights it like that same truck driver now in his caffeine crash. Sophie is sure that her time would be best spent continuing to smile and laugh and impart her baby wisdom. But I know better. I know that any second, the baby beauty will become a monster beast, so I am determined to put said baby down for a nap before the ugly transformation occurs.

Sweet Sophie cuddles in my arms until we approach her bedroom and I start closing the blinds; then she cries as if she's been in this torture chamber before, and she can't, just can't have her toes broken again.

I try some sweet talk, which is rejected with vehement protestations, and so I gently release the writhing, screaming banshee into the crib. She peers up at me, one tiny baby tear falling down her face, with an expression that says, "How could you do such a horrid, horrid thing to me?" The look is so scathing, laced with hurt, that I avert my eyes and whisper, like the coward that I am, "Nighty night, have a good nap!" and race out of there as if being attacked by a host of hungry hornets.

Then the wait begins. Generally, the screams last less than a minute. I stand in the kitchen as if I'm baking or cleaning, but actually I'm just listening attentively. The next two minutes are low-pitched complaints. "Gr pla koey dkod." I don't want to even guess what she's saying about me.

And finally silence. Now that I'm a seasoned grandmother I know better, but before, as a newbie, I used to tiptoe in after just five minutes of silence and look down at the little angel, sound asleep. Until suddenly, she'd open her huge blue eyes, send a look to me like "Aha!" and jump on her knees, rewinding her protests from just a short while earlier.

Now, in my learned wisdom, I find something to do for at least eight minutes. THEN I tiptoe into my granddaughter's room, ears pricked for any sound other than the soft sighs of a sleeping baby. If all is clear, I avoid the creaking floorboards and stand on the rug, looking at this new human being who sleeps as if she lives in paradise.

Her arms are flung above her head in complete comfort. Ah, to have shoulders like that once more. Her chubby legs are covered in a soft fuzzy blanket up to her chin. Her mouth puckers into a pink rosebud. Long eyelashes curl over her softly closed eyes, and I thank God for the opportunity to witness this sleeping bundle of love.

Joy

WE GREET EACH OTHER WITH SERENE SOFT SMILES.

"How was yours?"

"Fantastic. How was yours?"

"Unbelievable. I never had one of these before. This is so amazing." Another smile and I laugh.

A special day out, just the two of us, away from other family members and work and stress and the daily detritus of living.

We walk slowly to the locker room, touching each other's faces. "Wow, yours is so soft," she whispers.

I peer into the large, round blue eyes of my daughter. Everything about her is soft—her lips, her smile, her heart. I touch her skin. "And warm," I reply.

"Hot towels. The lady placed these hot towels over my neck and my cheeks and my forehead until only my mouth, nose, and eyes were exposed. It's rainy and windy and cold outside. Do you know how good that felt?"

I giggle. "Not to mention the heated sheets we lay on, and the flannel blanket on top of us."

"I didn't want to get up," my daughter, mother of three little ones, admits.

We stand in front of the mirror in the well-appointed locker room, checking out our newly puffed pink faces. Our eyes catch each other's during mid-primp, and we grin even wider.

Mother/daughter joy.

What Is It About Women and Their Feet?

"I REFUSE TO GO! NO ONE TOUCHES MY FEET!"

That was my mom's reaction when I stopped in front of a beautiful spa to give the female members in my East Coast family a treat. I had just spent seven hours in the car with my daughter and granddaughter to reach Delaware for some "Nanny" time.

My mom is the most put-together ninety-one-year-old you'll ever meet. She wears light blue and pink pastel sweaters to show off her blue eyes and snow white hair. She shows off her lithe figure in Gap Kids jeans. Her earrings always match her necklace, which matches the color of the sweater she's selected for the day.

She wears Converse sneakers to look cool—and to hide her feet.

What is it about us women and our feet?

My seven-year-old granddaughter runs around the backyard shoeless even in November, enjoying the feel of the bare earth on her sweet little toes. But by the time we're seventeen, we wear shoes that squish our feet into narrow tubes and raise our heels to a height no foot, no matter how sexy, should ever aspire to.

Men know better. They wear flats from the age of 1 to 101.

But women? Like Cinderella's stepsisters, we push, cajole, and squeeze our naturally wide/plump/happy/fleshy feet into leather devices of torture.

And then we try to walk in them.

I'll never forget when my 15-going-on-25-year-old niece once tried to explain to her dad why women walked in wounded pain every day. "It's for the sex," she said to my wide-eyed brother. "High heels raise the female rear end, which entices the male."

Enticing or not, by the age of forty, we women do everything we can to hide our bunions, blisters, and other unnatural foot disasters caused by the wrong (sexy?) shoe.

Bunions and hammertoes grow with age, so by the time we're, well, of a certain age, women's feet can look rather monstrous. Thus, we hide them.

In flat shoes!

A pedicure can soothe the sores, massage the ankles, and assuage the canker in our cantankerous toes. Thus, I figured a visit to a savory spa with our four-female-generation posse on this gloomy November weekend would be a perfect proposition.

Until my mom put both feet on the ground in brake position and refused to move. Thankfully, my little granddaughter looked up at her great-grandmother and said as sweet as sugar, "Please, Nanny?"

With a pout and a fear that the staff would gasp in horror once she took her shoes off, my mom put one foot in front of the other and entered the building. Once her feet settled into the warm, bubbly tub of scented water, her pout turned to a huge sigh of comfort.

The pedicure became a feat of feet-appreciation.

It only took ninety-one years to get there.

THREE
Life is Funny

Burnt Toast

True, we were rushing.

"Hurry up!" I exclaimed to my guy as he jumped into the shower. We'd told our friends we'd pick them up at 8:15 this Sunday morning to get an early start to our two-day hiking trip. We had all been getting to the point of feeling burnt out. A perfect time to get away, clear the cobwebs in our heads, and enjoy some fresh air in God's country.

I pulled the lever down on my super-duper one-year-old stainless steel toaster in the kitchen, then dashed back to the bedroom where my suitcase was half-packed. But I also cleaned up the dog's hair on the chair (that he never sits on, oh no, never), closed the windows, made the bed, and jotted down notes for the dogsitter.

That's when I smelled it. Burnt … toast? Then I saw the smoke swirling toward me, like a monster sneaking out of a blue lagoon. Only in this case, creeping throughout the condo.

Running back to the kitchen like a madwoman, I cringed at the smoke belching out of that newfangled toaster—and, did I see some flames too? I unplugged it, but then swore, not so softly. An alarm was screeching so loudly that it could wake up our neighbors.

Wait. The screaming alarm didn't come from our place, but from the outside hallway, connected to each of the six condo units. Shit, Shit, Shit.

I knocked on the bathroom door and walked in. "Um," I said sweetly to my guy through the shower door, "We have a little problem."

I quickly opened all the windows in every room of the condo on my way to our front door. Wait, I realized my attire was not appropriate for anyone other than the dog and the husband. Hurried to the closet, buttoned up a long winter coat, and opened the door to discover two neighbors, men who lived in two different units, standing in front of the offending alarm: one in his velour bathrobe, the other in tennis shorts so tiny they had to be from the 1970s. You know, Jimmy Connors-style.

I gulped, then apologized, "All my fault. Bad toaster."

They couldn't have been nicer. Or more understanding. Even when the fire truck roared up the driveway and three burly yellow-slickered, yellow-rubber-booted firemen bounced out of the truck over to the alarm, where my shirtless, red-shorted husband now also stood, looking at the large clanging button as if wondering if a sledgehammer would shut it up.

Within minutes, the siren was killed and all six men stomped through our condo to check up on the smoke. Did you know that you should NOT open all the windows when smoke is invading every inch of the place?

Now you do.

"Just open up one window, then it doesn't go into every room," the cute, muscled younger-than-my-son fireman explained to me. Then he stared at my winter coat.

It was 70 degrees outside.

I shrugged, they left, and our friends waited patiently for their pick up. I texted, "Burnt toast."

They texted back, "Better than burnt out. Breathe. Smile. Relax!"

And thus, the weekend began.

Adventures in Babysitting

MY BOSTON GRANDDAUGHTER VISITS MY MAN AND ME IN THE BAY AREA FOR a wonderful wacky week, but now it's time for me to fly her back to the "right" coast.

Because of a planned 6:30 a.m. shuttle for a 9:00 a.m. flight, I urge my rosebud to bed early the night before and warn her, "I'll wake you up tomorrow so we can make our flight on time!"

Every other morning, the sleepy princess slumbers past 8:30, and her devious grandmother (yes, that's me), anxious for the day's fun to begin, releases the button on her air mattress, deflating the bed and waking the befuddled girl.

So on flight day, I wake up at 5:00 a.m., figuring I have seventy-five minutes to shower, dress, and pack before the little one is awake.

But at 5:15, I hear a noise in the child's room and find her dressed (including headband, shoes, and bracelet), ready to "help" her Madre.

Have you ever packed with a five-year-old? Each item is lovingly petted, then thrown into the suitcase with wild abandon. The child practices bouncing and jumping on the said suitcase so that it closes properly.

However, her red carry-on case is cajoled to close too aggressively, and one of the side locks suddenly appears in the girl's hand. Her wide blue eyes express the perfect sentiment: *Whoops.*

We swirl to the airport and stand in line at security, me handling my suitcase, her suitcase, my carry-on and her carry-on, while simultaneously holding granddaughter's hand.

The line is long, the wait interminable for a wide-awake little girl. "Mommy always lets me sit on my carry-on," she explains patiently.

Well, Mommy wasn't missing a lock, I mumble to myself, but for the sake of happiness, I let my sweetuns sit (softly! I admonish) on her hard red case.

But the damn lock is missing, and with ten people ahead of us, and ninety-eight behind, the red case explodes open.

Out pop 6 My Little Ponies; 1 toothbrush; 4 headbands; 1 long-legged, pink-clad doll; 3 Fancy Nancy books; and 1 kid's medical kit that includes a stethoscope, blood pressure cuff, thermometer, and reflex hammer.

The security guard barks, "Keep it moving!" as I frantically throw the items, now spread out on the airport floor like ants on a picnic table, into the red case.

"Hurry, Madre," my granddaughter exclaims, probably hearing the exasperated sighs behind us.

Miraculously, I jam it all in and snap the case (sort of) shut, leaving out not even one little pony.

We make it to our airplane seats unimpeded, although I admit my grateful sigh is loud enough to induce some chuckles in the rows in front and behind us. I pray that the little one is as tired as I am after our early morning trials, but she proceeds to talk, and talk, and talk the entire five-and-a-half-hour trip! Not that her conversation isn't fascinating, but halfway through I suggest it's time for us to take a nap.

I could have suggested we take a flying leap out of the airplane at 3,000 feet in the air. "Madre! Did you forget I don't nap anymore?!"

Two hours later I suggest we close our eyes, just to give them a rest.

"I'm not tired, Madre, but you can close your eyes." She proceeds to examine me with her medical kit, stethoscope on my chest and thermometer on my lips, to see if there is a medical reason for my fatigue.

And then, she asks to go to the bathroom, noting that the "pilots" seem to walk to the rear of the plane often (she doesn't understand the difference between flight attendants and pilots, and I'm so impressed that she thinks it's normal to have three female pilots for one plane, I don't try to explain).

But when we make it to the back, my granddaughter is shocked and dismayed at the "pilots" sitting in their seats, facing the wrong way.

"HOW CAN THEY STEER FROM HERE???" she screams in concern.

Philosophically, I think sometimes that's exactly how it feels in life—we steer from the wrong end of the plane.

But I ditch my ruminations, buy her a ginger ale and a box of raisins, and we read "The Night Before Kindergarten" until the plane gently lands.

Facing the right way.

Contracts, Audrey Hepburn, and Miracles

"The contract will be ready to sign at 3:00, darling. I'm sorry it's taken so long. But my dear, it's here. The owner is ready for you to add your signature to his. He wants you to...."

"Umm," I interrupt on the phone in my normal elegant manner. "Uh, I don't...."

"You don't want to start the first of the month, my friend. I understand that." The Persian-born realtor spoke deeply-accented and swiftly, interspersing her words with endearments that made me blush.

"So my sweet being," she continues. "No worries. The start date is the middle of the month. Just hop into that cute little car of yours in an hour, and we'll see you...."

"But three o'clock doesn't quite work," I explain, expanding my voice more authoritatively. Then I squeak out, "Four?"

"My love, my sweet beauty, 4:00 is too late for the owner. He's gone by 4:00. He drove all this way just to meet you and sign the contract."

I imagine that the realtor's large, darkened eyebrows move closer together, her lips beginning to pout.

"I know, I'm sorry," I sigh, "but I have this other appointment. Three o'clock is difficult."

"Deeficult?" Oh my, now her eyebrows are probably on top of her forehead. "You have been calling me twice a day for this property. You have pleaded and begged and, little one, my good, good friend, I've worked for you. I've made this happen for you, my love. Three o'clock, you be here. Yes?"

I first met this woman two weeks ago, so I'm flattered that I'm now her good, good friend. Are we close enough, in the kingdom of female friendship, for me to tell her why three o'clock is impossible?

"Azra," I whisper, praying that I'm saying her name correctly. "Azra, I've needed a manicure for fifteen days now. FIFTEEN days! My fingernails are ragged. This deal has devastated my nail beds, not to mention my cuticles."

Silence.

Have I gone too far?

"Darling. Why didn't you say so? Of course you must get your nails fixed. I'll hold him off, Mr. Big Owner. I'll ply him with cookies and whatever. You come, with gleaming nails. I'll see you at 4:00, my pretty sweet pea."

I hang up the phone with a smile and think of Audrey Hepburn.

I believe in manicures. I believe in overdressing. I believe in primping at leisure and wearing lipstick. I believe in pink. I believe happy girls are the prettiest girls. I believe that tomorrow is another day, and... I believe in miracles.

— AUDREY HEPBURN

Whistle While You Work

I can't whistle.

I used to try, when I was a young girl, attempting to imitate my dad. His light-hearted whistle always made my heart jump. I felt happy, joyful, like everything was right in our world.

But I finally gave up about the time I began wearing "training" bras. Whistling was a part of childhood to discard, like my favorite stuffed dog and a 7:00 p.m. bedtime.

Then, as a mom, I tried to teach my progeny, pursing my lips together, blowing out spittle, never succeeding. My children were just as genetically disabled, so the entire family gave up whistling years ago.

Until the joy of whistling returned to me early one morning this summer, when the boxes had been packed and the furniture readied. The clock struck eight times, and a large moving van arrived with four men to load and drive our possessions to a new place, two minutes away.

I liked the condo my man and I had lived in for two years (lease ended, owner putting it on the market), so all the time and effort necessary to start anew at another place was disheartening.

Until the movers arrived.

Except for one wiry man in his forties, the other well-muscled fellows were twenty-five and younger. They arrived fresh faced and attentive, despite the morning hour and the heavy load ahead of them. They talked little, nary a grunt from anyone, and worked in a synchronicity that looked balletic.

And then.

A whistle.

The dark-haired kid with one earring, a small goatee, and legs thicker than tree trunks began to whistle. You know, like a dwarf in Snow White, whistling while he worked.

Happily!

Gaily!

Loudly!

My spirit soared. This move would be just fine. We'd love our new place, my man and I, and we'd have fun unpacking everything and finding new ways to arrange the sofa and the tea kettle, the family photos and the hummingbird feeder, the computer table and the reading chair.

I smiled, pursed my lips, and … couldn't conjure even the hint of a sound.

But that was okay. Jason the mover brought a whistle into my head, and that's all I needed to sing happily all move long.

Perhaps we should all whistle while we work, even if it's soundlessly.

Fear of (Not) Flying

I'M NOT A FLYER.

As passengers stand in line to board the plane (after they've all scurried like scared squirrels to have tickets checked, hurrying through the tunnel just to stand and wait), I stay behind.

I do not want to enter that metal tube until absolutely necessary.

I'm not afraid of the actual flying part. I understand the physics of how the plane's engines boost us up into the sky, the dynamics of keeping us up there, the mechanism of getting us, and the plane, down in one piece.

That's the easy part. The difficulty, for me, is being squished in that flying tube with 200 other people, with nowhere to go. What if I decide, mid-flight, that I really don't want to be up there? That, in fact, I want to touch Earth, now, and walk a mile or so to stretch my legs, or maybe find a burger joint and eat real food, or, even more possibly, go pee someplace more private than a three-inch by three-inch box with a suspiciously sticky floor and tiny sink full of used water and strands of hair.

What do I do then?

I hyperventilate. Sweat pours off my forehead and down my back. My skin gets itchy, my lungs get smaller, and my heart starts racing even faster than the jet. My mouth opens so I can scream, "Let me out!" but my brain takes over and demands, "Shut up, Pam."

Most times, my brain wins over. I grab my paperback and delve into the story, urging my thoughts to go there, into the characters' setting, into their dilemmas and fears, so I can ignore mine.

But sometimes, my desire for freedom (read: my claustrophobia), wins.

Like the time my man and I meander off one large plane knowing we have a three-hour wait for the next (much smaller) plane to reach our vacation destination, but are told we can rush to the gate and make an earlier flight instead. We're elated—we can get to the beach, and a drink, even sooner!

But we're the last ones on the plane, and the flight attendant points us to our seats—in the last row. Gamely, I follow my guy down the aisle, talking to myself all the way "You'll be fine, just 30 minutes, suck it up."

Until we sit down, the flight attendant starts her safety spiel, and I pop up like a broken jack-in-the-box (in this case, Pam-in-a-box) and literally run back up the aisle to freedom. I dimly hear my dear seatmate shout, "Where are you going?" and the attendant yell, "But the door's already closed." I don't care. I Am Getting Out of There.

As I pass Row 5, a passenger on the aisle grabs my arm softly and whispers, "It's okay," treating me like a wild horse and she the horse whisperer. "I'll switch," she continues, urging me to take her seat while she trudges down, down, down the narrow aisle to sit next to my bemused mate.

Thus, not only do I make it to our vacation island still married (to an understanding man), but my love for all humanity has tripled.

Nonetheless, every time my guy and I travel together, he holds my hand a bit too firmly as we enter the plane and sit in our (as-close-to-the-front-as-possible) seats. But there's no need for him to hold tight.

I realize that my biggest fear now is not "flying," but "not flying," and thus missing out on visiting enchanting people, like grandchildren, and exotic places, like New Jersey.

Currently my mantra as I enter a plane is:

"It's the destination, not the journey!" (Apologies to Siddhartha)

Under the Princess Canopy

To my four-year-old granddaughter, the most exciting part of my visit is that I get to sleep with her in her queen-sized bed.

At 9:30 p.m., Sophie's constant energy is barely contained, even with the lights out and flannel sheets up to our chins. The bed is crowded with just the two of us, since half a dozen "My Little Ponies" have joined us on the counterpane, jumping in high spirits at my presence.

The chatter between Sophie and her tiny plastic friends finally turns to whispers, and then soft little snores. I start to fade out myself until I'm poked on one hip by a pony fairy wing, and I feel a plastic tail wiggle in my ear. Quietly, I place all the fantastical toys in the bin on the floor and sink back into comfortable oblivion.

Until my eyes pop open. Two little-girl feet are propped on my face. I raise my neck a few inches and notice the sleeping child's head down at the foot of the bed.

Not wanting to wake her (I really do believe in letting sleeping ponies, and little girls, lie), I slowly twist away and gently move the child's knees off my chest.

An hour later (or is it only minutes?), an arm whaps me on the neck, and then a precious child, now right-side up, cuddles into my stomach, finding my body a useful pillow.

I stare at the wispy white princess canopy over my head and demand my brain to stop laughing and GO BACK TO SLEEP.

Which I do, until an errant dolly finds my lower back, and brilliant little Sophie begins talking in her sleep.

Mathematical equations?

Poetry?

An arcane language?

Oh. She's mumbling about "glimmer winged" pony Rainbow Dash chasing Fluttershy in the magical night air.

5:00 a.m. and I just lie on the soft bed with my sweet grandchild, pretending that winged ponies are flying in and out of the canopy, dusting us with glitters of grandmotherly love.

No RE-lax at LAX

WHEN I FIRST ENTER THE LAX (LOS ANGELES AIRPORT) TERMINAL I'M immediately bombarded with a mass of humanity. Where did everyone come from? Well, literally, from Hong Kong and Chicago, Honolulu and New York, Singapore and … but I digress.

Besides the fact that thousands of men, women, children, and babies are strewn throughout the airport like fish trying to swim upstream, I note that no one looks (dare I say it without sounding extremely naïve?) … friendly.

My guy and I escape to, hopefully, more amiable rooms at the Admiral's Club, where those with American Airline points (and a club membership) can get away from the general riffraff and re-lax in peace. Sure enough, the men and women here scowl silently. Their heads are lowered to their cell phones or iPads or laptops. I search for long minutes to find someone talking to someone else.

Wait—out of the fifty or so people sitting on leather chairs and couches and tall café stools, I do see half a dozen conversing. On their phones. To someone not in the same room as they are.

Okay, perhaps I'm being too cynical. Somebody must be smiling. Somewhere.

My tired eyes (our flight was over five hours) scan the room and the bar, where a ten-year-old kid carries a glass of red wine to some adult not nearby. An attractive mid-twenties woman, wearing a tight red sweater, tighter black leggings, and stiletto-heeled black boots, seemingly talks to herself as she munches on pretzels. I assume she's wearing little earpieces in her diamond-studded ears. Many important-looking men carry worry lines between their eyebrows like a badge of honor.

I quietly scoot two rooms away to the "Ladies Room." A few nice-looking women (Hollywood stars, perhaps? though I don't recognize anyone) primp in front of the mirror. After washing my hands, I search for the paper towels. Oh, there they are, above the box labeled "Disposable Needles."

WHAT?

I want to escape this Alice-in-Wonderland hole, frantically waving to my guy that it's time for us to leave. His quizzical expression makes me laugh until I see the ten-year-old kid sipping from the glass of red wine.

I grab my spouse's hand and catch a beautiful beam from the janitor, a tiny man with gleaming teeth, as he washes the glass exit doors.

There.

A smile.

One person knows how to RE-LAX in LAX.

I'm flying out of there before I get stuck in the rabbit hole called LA.

Scammed

I'm home making dinner and my cell phone rings.

I check the number and groan. Scammers now send calls using the same area code and first three digits of a nearby town. In my case, each call says "Groton."

I ignore the call and sauté the onions before the phone rings again. And, three minutes later, again.

Just about ready to throw the phone into the drawer and lock it up, I notice that the "scammer" has left a voice mail message. Weird. Scammers never leave a "calling card," so to speak.

I listen. A young voice says, "Hi Margery. This is Clark. I just want you to know that I have a …." The voice hesitates and I hear a female respond in the background. The mother, I guess, and then the young person adds, "a gizmo for my birthday. Call me back!"

Oh, I think, how cute. This kid thinks he's calling Margery, whoever she is—a friend of the family? And wants to tell her all about his gizmo. Whatever that is. And the kid's name is Clark, just like my grandson's.

I feel sorry that the young boy thinks he's left a message for Margery, and Margery will never answer. So, I return the call. The young voice answers with an uncertain "Hello?"

"Hi!" I say. "You left a message for Margery. I am not Margery. You got the wrong number."

Stunned silence on the other end. Then the boy says, "Ohhhhh kayyyyy," sounding immensely confused.

"Bye!" I hang up, feeling unsettled.

Ten seconds later, my phone rings again with a number I recognize—my daughter's. "Hello!" I say liltingly.

"Mom. Why did you tell Clark you're not his Madre?"

My heart sinks toward my wobbly knees. "That was Clark?"

"Yes, he told you he was Clark."

"But I thought he asked for Margery." As the words flew out of my mouth, I realized he asked for me, his Madre. "Well, why is the phone number from Groton?" I ask, trying to defend myself.

I hear my daughter's exasperated sigh. "It's the phone number for his Gizmo—you know, a smart watch for kids."

I want to tell her she is speaking gibberish. I want to tell her that I thought I'd been scammed. I want to tell her that back in the day, gizmo meant an object whose name you couldn't recall. Instead I say, "Could you please put Clark on the phone?"

Thank goodness my nine-year-old grandson has a sense of humor. "I got worried when you told me you weren't my Madre," he confesses with a smile in his voice. "Can I call you now on my Gizmo?"

FOUR

For the Dogs

My Dog Is a Zen Master

I ARRIVE HOME AT LUNCHTIME WITH A THIRTY-MINUTE BREAK FROM WORK. I am hassled and frazzled and tired. I dump some leftovers into a saucepan while washing the breakfast dishes, starting a load of laundry, and cleaning up the newspapers scattered on the dining room table.

That's when I see the patch of sunlight, and the yogi.

He can't cross his legs as human meditators do, but instead sits like a Sphinx, front legs straight ahead, his beautiful gold and white furry chest held straight and proud. His neck rises a bit as he faces me and holds my green eyes with his chocolate brown ones. The expression is wise and all-knowing, and I can hear his thoughts immediately:

Why don't you calm down, for heaven's sake?

The sun is basking his body in heat and light, and his mouth opens to pant. But actually he is trying to say something to me, like:

Stop. Look. Listen. Life is only this. Stop. Look. Listen.

The timer buzzes, but I ignore it and sit down next to my dog, stroking the warm fur. I feel the sun melt my tense muscles, my frayed nerves, and my buzzing brain. I breathe deeply and . . .

Stop

Look

Listen

Slowly, I also become one with the day.

At least for a few minutes.

Searching for Your "People"

LAST NIGHT I WENT TO BED EARLY TO FINISH A GOOD BOOK, LEAVING HENRY (the dog) and the other man of the house watching TV in the family room. Suddenly I heard Henry bark. It wasn't his "I have to go out" bark, or "Where's my dinner" bark, but his "Help! I can't find you, where are you?" bark.

I laughed and called for him, and he came bouncing to me happily, tail wagging as if I'd been lost and finally found.

His reaction reminded me of how important we are to each other—"we" meaning our family members, our good friends, our "people."

Almost two years ago, Henry and my guy and I moved cross country, driving in our SUV over eight hours a day, Henry sprawled out in the back seat, happier than a clam in mud. After all, he had us, "his people," alone in a small moving box for hours at a time. For once, he always knew where we were. He'd lift his head from the little cave we'd built him with blankets, his water bowl, and a ball, and his smile so wide I realized that he'd be happy if we all lived in the car forever.

But within six days we arrived at Truckee, our last stop before reaching the S.F. bay area. Reservations had been made at the "dogs allowed" hotel, and we were relieved to find our room on the first floor near the exit door and a good walking path.

Henry sniffed at his new spot for the night, a bit anxious that it smelled differently than the night before. My guy made several trips to carry luggage and laptop and dog essentials from the car to the room, and then we unpacked the necessities, as had become our routine.

Until we heard an anxious bark outside our room from far away, and then another, and another.

"It is a dog-friendly hotel," we remarked to each other, smiling and looking for Henry's perked ears and curious eyes.

But Henry was not there. He was gone! We searched the corners of the room, the bathroom, the closet.

The outside barks became more insistent. "Where are you?" the bark said. "Where are you?"

"Oh my God!" I exclaimed. "That's Henry's bark!"

We yanked open our hotel door. Way down the lengthy hotel hallway, we saw a yellow blur. Our nine-year-old golden was running up and down the long corridor, barking outside each door, shouting, "Where are you?"

"Henry, here!" I shouted. He flew toward us like a happy puppy, like a child who's momentarily lost a parent, like a person who has been reunited with his loved ones.

We had a sweet reunion with hugs and licks and a tail wagging so hard it hit the other side of the hallway, causing a couple of doors to open with inquisitive expressions from the rooms' residents.

"Our dog was lost in the hallway," we explained.

"Ah," the dog owners responded. "Now he's found his people."

Exactly.

Sharing the Divine

I CAN COMMUNICATE WITH ANIMALS.

Just last night, I stared straight into my golden retriever's eyes and said silently, "Henry, do you really like that plain yogurt I give you every night with your dinner?"

He stared back liquid pools of brown love and answered, *Anything you give me is full of love, and how can love not taste divine?*

I sat back in my chair, stunned.

I wasn't surprised that I'd heard Henry's words as clearly as a train whistle, or a fog horn, or a hummingbird's wings. His words have rung loudly other times, although I admit the phenomenon is rare.

Most times I feel his answer; if you've never communicated with an animal, you don't know what I mean. But some dog or cat lovers are nodding their heads. We humans usually don't like to admit that there's a language bond between species, probably because humans own the ridiculous assumption that we're superior to every other being.

No, I wasn't shocked because he answered me, but instead taken aback by his words.

DIVINE.

Food and love, giving and receiving, cooking and eating, all are part of the Divine. With a capital D.

I raced to the kitchen, where earlier I'd placed half a dozen Meyer lemons from a friend's garden. Henry watched me, knowingly, a little drool appearing on the side of his black gums.

I started measuring sugar, cracking eggs, pouring flour into a bowl, turning the mixer to full speed, then allowing the dog to lick the beaters as his special treat.

Lemon bars. Cooling now on the rack, ready to share with others.

Divine.

Oxen Mystic

I WOKE UP IN THE MIDDLE OF THE NIGHT AS SICK AS A DOG. WAIT. MY DOG never got this sick. Henry, my golden, had the constitution of an ox and the compassion of a mystic, so he woke up and followed me as I raced to the bathroom.

I don't remember what happened next, except when I awakened I had a huge headache, an even bigger lump on my head, and someone breathing into my nose.

I had not only fainted, I must have had a seizure (rare, but an occurrence if my body gets stressed). I lay flat on the cold tile bathroom floor; just lifting my head caused me to groan. The dizziness was overwhelming. I could not get up. My husband was on a business trip, and my bed and phone were miles away.

But not Henry. His face covered mine, and then he licked me from stem to stern. "Stop," I moaned. His tongue was long and wet and cold. I began to shiver. Henry would have nothing to do with my protestations. Once he explored my skin and found no blood, he knew what to do to protect me.

He plopped on top of me. The warmth of his body settled mine. I didn't want him there, and I shouted for him to leave. But he never wavered, except for getting up once in a while to peer into my eyes. *Was I okay?*

After three hours, I finally crawled from bathroom to bed and climbed up onto the bed, burrowing into the sheets. I slept for hours and when I woke up mid-morning, hours later than Henry's own pee time and break-fast, he sat upright next to the bed, staring into my eyes. *Are you okay?* he asked, licking my face.

No. I pulled my phone close and called my daughter for help. Henry never left my side until she arrived and, even then, he'd never peed so fast, forsaking his meal to plop right by my side again.

More mystic than ox, I decided.

Walking the Human

I'M HAPPY TO GREET YOU ALL AS A GUEST AUTHOR. MY BEST FRIEND (BF AS I affectionately call her) is too frazzled with preparations for the holiday to write. So I get to put in my two cents here, or in my case, two kibbles.

During this season, I try to calm my BF down, explain the true meaning of the holiday, blah, blah, blah, but she still frantically bakes cookies, shops, wraps gifts, and attends too many parties.

I must admit I also enjoy the excitement and extra vibe in the air, and love the anticipation of the big day when Santa arrives. After all, I have my own stocking (didn't you know that Santa loves dogs?). I was given a green felt collar with tinkling bells, but fortunately my BF doesn't make me wear it.

The good news is that with all the baking, my BF feels she needs to walk extra miles to burn off the calories, and that's just fine by me. I take her for a walk as often as humanly possible (it's always possible for a dog to walk). My other dog friends and I laugh when we hear our best friends say that they're going to "take the dog for a walk." None of us have allowed our BFs to walk us since we were puppies—we take them for a walk, and train them the best we can.

For instance, my BF reads poetry and recites quotes about "stopping to smell the roses," but while walking, she only wants to "keep up the pace" and check her pedometer. I, on the other paw, understand the meditative pleasure of stopping to sniff the bushes. It's been a tough lesson to teach, but I'm patient with her and hope that one of these days, she'll get it.

In the meantime, I hear the mixer mashing up some butter and sugar in the next room, so I'll send my goodbyes quickly. I'm a good companion in the kitchen and sit by my BF's feet whenever cooking commences. She says I'm too close and she'll trip over me, but I know that, really, she loves my company. As a reward for my loyalty, my BF makes sure I get a lick of batter at the end.

And that's my wish for you and all your kind. May you always get to lick the batter, sniff the bushes, and enjoy the company of your BF.

Early Morning Spirits

I'M WALKING THE SAME PATHS AS I DID WHEN HENRY SNIFFED ALONG WITH ME. Days after he died, when I began walking alone, I realized how much of a fixture we had become on those early morning walks. Half a dozen other early ramblers inquired, "Where's Henry?" or "Where's that bright-eyed, bushy-tailed dog of yours?"

Now it's almost five months later, and I still walk our same route. This morning, one of Henry's biggest fans stops me on the path, San Francisco Bay on one side, a tiny otter face peeking out of the foggy mist.

"So, are you getting a new dog?" the woman asks. I don't know her name, but she knows my dog's name. Every time she speed-walked past us in dog-days-past, she nodded knowingly at Henry's hippy limp, his dragged leg, and said to him, "I'm right there with you, kid. You're my inspiration."

Henry was twelve at the time, about eighty-four in human years. The same as her age.

"No," I answer now. "I'm still missing him too much." I pause, wondering if I should go on, but the lady's eyes have not left mine. "I still feel him around me, even see him in the dark of night," I confess.

The older woman nods her head. "My husband has been gone for five years," she says. "I still talk to him, and he still answers."

I swallow hard. "Well, I still talk to Henry, and believe it or not, I still feel his thoughts. Crazy, huh?"

The woman places her soft delicate hand on my arm. "No, it's not crazy. A dog's spirit is as much alive as a human's."

"Well," I reply, ready to resume my walk. "That's why I'm not ready to get another dog."

She chuckles and begins to walk in the opposite direction, calling out as she does, "I know. That's why I never got another husband."

Henry smiles along with me as we finish our last mile.

FIVE

The Extraordinary Ordinary

Open-Mouthed Kisses

I WANT TO BLAME SOMEONE FOR THE HORRIBLE COLD I GOT LAST WEEK. MY SON is first on the list. We met for lunch in the city the week before. He was sneezing and sniffling and suggested we shouldn't hug hello or goodbye. But how do you not hug someone you love?

Two days later I still felt just fine. Then I worked at the town's Holiday Art and Craft Sale, where friends and strangers are all in the holiday spirit and shake hands and laugh and sip on warm spiced cider. After each hand I shook I shuddered—how many germs in that one little shake? I'm not mysophobic, although these days we're all being bombarded with movies and stories and news articles about "the big virus epidemic" sure to come. [Author's note, this was written before January 2020].

How can we not cringe when we're flying in a steel tube with 200 strangers and the one sitting next to us coughs loudly enough to rattle the entire plane? Yuck! Or when we open a door to a bank or restaurant, following the germy handprints of dozens of others? Or when a well-meaning customer comes into the office with a smile and a warm moist handshake?

But I believe in being friendly, so I don't give an air pump or a touchless high five to the sweet neighbor who drops by with a plate of cookies, or the fireman who helps me, once again, turn off my smoke alarm. I give hugs.

Some people are now into the "touch-free" hugs. Remember the "air kiss," a kind of European sweep to one cheek, purse lips but no contact, stand back and move to the other cheek? I see friends, mostly female, air kiss all the time. Maybe it's the new hug of the future. Maybe it's not a bad idea.

But it looks ... unfriendly. Dare I even say, kind of fake?

Ah, now I realize whom I need to blame for my horrible terrible no-good sneezing coughing sore throat cold.

My sweet runny-nosed eighteen-month-old grandson.

He knows how to greet someone and make them feel special. Just a year and a half into this world, he's figured out that to melt the heart of a human and own her forever, give her a kiss and a hug. But he doesn't give them out indiscriminately. If you've shown him a good time, and maybe read him a book, played race car demon with him for an hour, and offered him a warm gooey chocolate chip cookie, then he dispenses that most precious reward.

The only problem is that he hasn't figured out how to kiss close-mouthed.

So yes, I spent some time with the toddler on the Friday before "the cold," and when it was time for him to go home, he opened up his little arms and said, "Me me, kee," (interpreted as "Pammy, Kiss!"). While his mother held him, he leaned way out toward me and met my lips with a large wet "O" of a baby mouth. After a happy loud "MOWM" sound, as if he'd just eaten a piece of high-end dark chocolate, he leaned back into his mom's arms with an expression of serenity and happiness.

Did I mention he had a cold?

But I wouldn't give up that open-mouthed kiss for all the germ-free touchless hugs in the world.

Would you?

Buttercups, Bollywood, and World Peace

LAST WEEKEND I ATTENDED A WEDDING AT WHICH I BARELY KNEW THE BRIDE and groom, yet I left the reception thinking of world peace.

My guy's brother's daughter, just finishing her fourth year of med school, married her college sweetheart, a handsome brown-eyed MBA grad, in their New England college chapel.

The Irish-Italian bride was gorgeous, all wide-eyed and lithe in her white lace gown. The Indian groom was svelte and handsome in his tux. Their splendid contrasts were highlighted by their family and friends: long and short dresses in reds, blacks, grays and purple on the bride's side, and even more colorful and sparkling saris on the groom's side.

I wondered about the tradition of a "bride's side" and a "groom's side" during the wedding, since it separated the two families, instead of integrating them.

The same lack of merging occurred as we were seated at the wedding reception, although I admit I was relieved to be sharing a table with my daughter and son-in-law, my man's siblings and spouses. No hard work required to talk to strangers.

But then the music began.

The DJ played loud and 60s. "Proud Mary," "Twist and Shout," "Bad Moon Rising," the Supremes, Rolling Stones, Beach Boys. By the third song, the dance floor was packed with pre-teen to 35-year-old cousins, mid-20s college pals, relatives from 40 to 80 years old, all whooping it up, raising arms as we sang "Shout!"

You know you make me wanna (SHOUT!)
Kick my heels up and (SHOUT!) (SHOUT BY ISLEY BROTHERS)

Cultures, colors, and creeds collided as over 100 people sang lyrics out loud, swinging hips and laughing during the next song—Buttercup:

Why do you build me up (Build me up) buttercup, baby
Just to let me down (Let me down) and mess me around
(BUILD ME UP BUTTERCUP, WRITTEN BY MIKE D'ABO AND
TONY MACAULAY, SUNG BY THE FOUNDATIONS)

As shoes got kicked off and saris twirled, I thought, now this is the way it's supposed to be.

Then suddenly the music changed to Bollywood songs, more formally known as Hindi film songs. Moving from oldies pop to Indian pop, no one broke stride.

Kate nahi katate yeh din yeh raat (These days and nights are not passing by)
Kehni thi tumse joh dil ki baat (I wanted to tell you what is there in my heart)
(KATE NAHI KATATE YEH DIN YEH RAAT, LYRICS BY JAVED AKHTAR)

Smiles grew even wider, strangers became dancing companions, and through it all I envisioned world peace.

One wedding at a time.

Loving Shrimp

I'M NOT THRILLED WITH SHRIMP.

I suppose they taste all right, but before cooked, they look like naked aliens. Or like the waste product of a whale.

So when my son-in-law announced, "I'm making shrimp stew for dinner," my stomach did a little "Oh shit," dance, but my mind leapt in joy and my lips blurted out, "Wow! That sounds delicious!"

Whatever he prepared, I would have responded as enthusiastically and happily for three reasons:

#1. He cooked so daughter Nadine and I, the special guest for the weekend, could sit around on the couch and drink wine while we watched. And on that Saturday night, my stomach would accept shrimp or lima beans or even sautéed liver, just because I was in the same room with my favorite New England family.

#2. While SIL cooked, my little grandchildren scampered in and out of the kitchen like soft fuzzy gerbils.

#3. And while the shrimp sizzled, my brother Chuck, whom I see once a year if I'm lucky since he lives in Maryland and I live in California, found a way to Boston, and to this N.E. family, for a quick twenty-four-hour visit.

The Cabernet he brought with him was too expensive: ruby red with expressions of cranberry and plum, which coated our mouths and minds like a soothing lubricant.

"My dog got in so much trouble this week," Chuck complained as he petted the family's sweet golden retriever. "He peed on the new rug, and he never misbehaves like that. I think he wanted to get in trouble."

"Why would he want to get in trouble?" I asked, nibbling on the salsa and chips I was offered.

"No dog, or man, wants to be perfect all the time," Chuck answered as if the comment made sense.

"Well, neither you nor my husband has a thing to worry about then," Nadine said with a laugh to her uncle.

I gulped some wine as I looked for SIL's reaction, but he was too busy chopping onions and green peppers and celery and throwing it all into his simmering tomato-based stew. Actually, right about then, he looked pretty perfect to me.

"I love shrimp," my normally non-effusive brother announced. In fact, the more wine I poured in his goblet, the more he loosened up and the wider he smiled. I could have hugged SIL for making a dish I wouldn't like, but that gave such joy to Chuck.

"I love shrimp too!" I said as I poured more wine into Dan's glass and clinked it with my own.

"Cheers!" we toasted to each other, to shrimp, and to ordinary family get-togethers that are extraordinary in their ability to make us happy.

Firm Support

I OPEN MY DRESSER DRAWER TO PULL OUT A BRA—MY FAVORITE ONE WITH THE lace and no underwire, just right for a day of writing and relaxation. My hand hovers over the array of other "stuff" in the drawer.

Among the three white bras and one black one, I shuffle through the small bag of potpourri; the sales tags from Nordstrom from three years ago; the tiny antique frame that needs to be mended, as it has for the four years it's sat in that drawer; and to the right, the pile of greeting cards.

Knowing I shouldn't, I pull the cards out. I hesitate, then put them back in their spot. I just do not have time to do this now. I look at the clock—8:12—and pull them out again. Okay, just a few.

The first one is a picture of bright yellow California poppies in a field. Last year's Mother's Day card from my son. I open it and smile. In his scrunched up, manly handwriting I read, "To an amazing person and an even more amazing mother. May you always know I appreciate everything you have done for me, and I love you very much." I feel tingly goose bumps roll up my spine. This time he didn't sign it with his first and last name, as in other years. Looking through my pile, I see his Mother's Day card from two years ago, and another from years before that.

Next I pull out a birthday card from my daughter. Last year? Two years ago? It's not dated, and I wish I had put a year on it. The cover of the orange, new-agey card proclaims, "I know a woman of strength and beauty. I have watched her for years." Inside, in script is added, "She is my mother. Happy Birthday." I feel my eyes water (as they do every time

I read the card), and then look at the added words, written with orange and blue magic markers. In blue she writes: "Mom, when I saw this card I immediately thought of you, because it says exactly what I think of you. I am blessed to not only know you, but to have you for my mom!"

The words from both my children never fail to touch me deep, deep down in my gut, and I allow myself a good cry for three minutes.

I have a pile of at least twenty cards I could go through, from husband, the kids, my mom, my dad, and friends, that remind me how extremely fortunate I am.

If I'm down and having a particularly tough day, I don't need to go to the medicine cabinet for a pill, a picker upper. I just go to my bra drawer.

That's where I always find lots of firm support.

Eating the Broccoli

I LOVE BROCCOLI AND FRESH GREEN BEANS. I LOVE CAULIFLOWER AND BRUSSELS sprouts, artichokes and corn, asparagus and spinach. Especially spinach.

But I didn't always. Remember when you were a kid, and your parents made you eat those obnoxious green, stringy, horrid, disgusting things called "vegetables"?

Why did we hate them so much? I remember plopping my peas into my glass of milk (whole milk, back in the day before the choices of non-fat or low fat) in order to hide them. Drip. Drop. Drip. One pea at a time. Thinking I'd get away with it. But my parents also made me finish my glass of milk every night. And surprise! A half dozen round peas lay in the bottom of my glass like tiny drowned smarmy green mice. My tears and histrionics drowned out the parental order: "Eat those mice or NO DESSERT!"

When did I learn to appreciate the finer aspects of the green goodies that help us stay lean and mean like a well-oiled machine? (Wasn't there an ad somewhere, sometime, like this for say, asparagus? If not, should have been.)

I can't remember eating spinach enthusiastically until I was pregnant with my first child. Then, I couldn't get enough of it. I'd stroll down the grocery aisles surreptitiously, sneaking into the freezer section, piling on boxes of frozen spinach one at a time, looking right and left to make sure no one saw. After all, who eats spinach voraciously like a wolf attacking red meat?

I'd rush home and start a small saucepan of boiling water, dropping in that iced square of green stringy stuff, timing the steaming impatiently, sighing with satisfaction as I gorged on the delicious delicacy with pure delight.

Some say my body craved iron; I say I just finally learned to let go of my prejudices and discover the goodness of vegetables.

Aldous Huxley once wrote: "The charm of history and its enigmatic lesson consist in the fact that, from age to age, nothing changes and yet everything is completely different." Same with broccoli and childhood. My grandchildren are now squirming through the difficulties of eating their vegetables. Sophie, three and a half years old, shows her quiet resolve to make it through this ordeal with good cheer as she "eats the broccoli" ... covered in ketchup.

Calm DOWN!

I HAVEN'T SEEN MY EAST COAST GRANDCHILDREN IN THREE MONTHS. MAYBE, at the ages of two and three, they won't remember me.

So, like any self-respecting, upright, honest, and upstanding woman, on this visit I bring two singing stuffed animals, two books, two lollipops, and a bag of my famous chocolate chip oatmeal bars.

They may not remember me, but by God, they will like me!

I arrive at their one-week vacation cottage, a place where they've never seen me, so they could be even more confused about who I am and how I fit into the scheme of things. But as soon as I enter the front door, I'm greeted with "Madre! Come see my room!" "Madre, look at my car!" "Madre, can I have my pop now?" "Madre, let's play outside!"

I breathe a sigh of relief as they cuddle with me, sit on my lap while I read stories, play with my sparkling earrings, and stroke my face like a blind person making sure my lips, eyes, and nose have remained in place.

But.

Still.

I want to be the good Madre, because after this week, I won't see them again for at least three more months.

So when they jump on the couch, I bite my lip.

When they eat their lollipops and touch the doorknobs with their sticky fingers, I only let an "ugh" escape.

When Sophie brushes my hair and pulls too hard on a curl, I just laugh.

Until bedtime.

The three of us are sharing the room—Sophie and I are in the double, Clark in his own little futon. The clock is pushing 10:00 and I'm spent, but Clark is yet again sneaking out of the room like a little munchkin looking for Oz.

"Clark!" I yell, scaring the poor kid into scampering back to his bed like a bird into his cage. "That's enough!" I continue. "Bed! Time!"

Sophie jumps out of her side of the bed and stands in front of me, chest puffed, hands held above her head.

"Madre, Madre!" she exclaims dramatically, moving her arms from the up position to below her waist. "C a l m D O W N! Just C A L M d o w n."

"But...!" I begin to protest. But then I realize, *What the hell, she's right!*

And I laugh.

And continue to be the good Madre the rest of the week.

The Weight of the Soul

"*BREATHE IN! BREATHE OUT.*

Breathe in and slowly move your chin to the right.

Exhale, back to center. Inhale, chin toward the right."

I slowly lead my chin, and my mind, into a trance. I'm so ready to leave this world and get transported by the words of my yoga teacher.

"Now inhale, move your head down, toward your chest."

Ah … I sigh. God that feels good.

"After all," the teacher explains soothingly, "the head weighs 15-20 pounds. That's…."

WHAT? My eyes pop open as they reach for the yogi's eyes. Is she kidding?

"Yes, yes," she says gently. "That's a lot of weight we carry on our neck."

I stop inhaling.

I stop exhaling.

My brain races with the thought. Twenty pounds? No wonder I can't lose weight. Those 20 pounds of pure brain tissue are keeping the scale unmoving, no matter that I gave up ice cream.

My body lists to the left. Oh shoot, I'm almost fainting because I've stopped breathing.

Inhale, Pam. Inhale.

But 20 POUNDS of brain? Why had I not considered this before? All the dreams and wishes and worries in there. All the love and hate (not much hate, but I really do dislike baked ham) in there. And the conversations—internally and then externally.

The soul—how much does the SOUL weigh, compared to the brain?

"Pam. Pam," the teacher looks grieved. "Where are you?"

I stand up straighter, swaying a bit from the lack of oxygen.

"I'm leaving," I announce.

I need to find someplace to weigh my head.

I float out the door, my head trailing behind, feeling heavier than ever before.

A Solitary Surprise

AH, TO BE ABLE TO GET AWAY BY MYSELF AND GO FOR A LONG SOLITARY WALK while my houseful of guests chatter and demand my attention in their sweet, non-demanding ways.

"Have to take the dog for a walk!" I shout out. Leash in hand, dog giving me a wonderful excuse, I nearly leap off the front stoop and race toward the wooded path just a few yards away. The leaves are beginning to turn, so I'm surrounded by mostly green hues tinged with yellows, a sudden brilliant red, an aggressive spray of orange. My spirits lift, and I think, *Alone at last, glory be.*

But at the next step, I hear a tinkling sound, like chimes, and as I follow the path, crunchy with fallen yellow birch leaves, the chiming becomes louder, more insistent.

Darn. My goal is to get away from civilization. What's this? The dog's ears perk up excitedly, and he drags me forward, even though I'd rather find another path.

Suddenly, we walk into a clearing where a small thatched-roof cottage sits unperturbed and peaceful. A curl of smoke rises from the chimney, and a glorious symphonic sound wafts from the open door. I step away, not wanting to disturb the occupant, but the dog races toward the door so excitedly that the leash pulls away from my hand. He has crashed the party, so to speak.

His tail disappears from the front entryway into the cottage. Mortified, I step up closer, my nose twitching at the delightful smell of freshly baked butterscotch muffins. My favorite! How strange. I raise my hand to knock on the open door, but a voice, strong yet husky and strangely familiar, shouts out, "Come in! Come in."

Prickles of surprise course up my spine into my scalp. I hear nothing from the dog. My stomach gurgles in hope, and my foot moves forward, despite my reservations.

I enter a room so cozy and soothing I want to sink into the nearest chair and stay forever. The space is filled with a few comfortable high-pillowed chairs and a loveseat covered in blue-flowered upholstery. The wood floor is covered with a soft blue chenille area rug. Red pillows and soft cashmere throws add a colorful accent to the inviting room, infused with light from three, large-paned windows.

A figure stands in the far doorway that leads to the kitchen. I can't identify her at first, she is bathed in afternoon light from the stained glass window that graces the top of the front door. But she moves slightly, and I gasp.

"Amazing, isn't it?" she says lightly.

I stare at the image of myself, standing as still as a statue while I regain my bearings. She is tall, 5 foot 7, with wavy blonde hair dotted with graying streaks. Her gray-green eyes are strong and direct, her full mouth pressed upward in a gentle smile.

It can't be.

She is exactly what I look like. She moves her head back and forth, as if to discourage me from trying to understand this phenomenon, and then she points toward one of the chairs.

"Have a seat. Let me tell you a story about life, and how little we know of what and who we really are."

I bolt out of that door faster than a rabbit released from a trap. Even while running, I ask myself, what am I so afraid of? Learning the truth? Or discovering that life has many divergent truths?

Either way, I'm a coward.

Ten minutes later, exhausted and out of breath, I stop. What have I done? I turn around, looking for the dog. He hasn't followed me. He's back there, at the cottage. I retrace my steps quickly, heart beating faster than I've ever allowed it to. My head spins with a thousand thoughts but only one question. Why did I run?

When I reach the spot, it is only a clearing with some low-hanging underbrush. No cottage. No smells of warm butterscotch muffins. No woman, and no dog.

I have lost my chance at discovery.

"Urf!" My dog is back, leashless, but smiling widely.

I agree with him. We have many solitary walks ahead of us, searching for that path to the answers.

SIX

Time Off

Spa STRESS

I SEIZE THE OPPORTUNITY TO ENJOY AN AFTERNOON AT THE SPA TO SPIFF UP AND stress down.

I succeed, sort of.

My visiting mother, always full of zip, is a bit reluctant, but my friend Rachel and I urge her to take time with us to R E L A X. So we arrive eagerly, quickly getting into the mood by wearing the spa's oversized plush robes as we sit in front of a warmed pool in the dazzling Sausalito sunshine.

We're each called away by our trained de-stressors. Mom's facialist is a warm Hawaiian woman who soothes her at "hellooooo." Rachel expects a woman masseuse, so when a handsome young man leads her to her massage, I whisper, "Just think 50 shades." The shocked blush-red expression on my friend's face starts me giggling, even as my massage begins—not the best way to let my muscles go limp. As strong fingers push open tight tender back muscles, my stomach bops up and down in suppressed laughter.

An hour later, warm lavender tea in front of a roaring fire as the fog swirls amidst the sun's rays continues the amazing effects of a splendid afternoon at the spa.

Until we're back in the car, coasting out of the driveway, and I think out loud, "Where's my cell phone?"

My foot hits the brake as my mind searches for the last time I used it.

Then I get a sinking feeling: "Oh NO!"

Just in case I'm wrong, I empty the contents of my purse and my book bag as Rachel, sitting in the passenger seat, calls my phone on her cell. She figures if we hear the ring, we'll find the phone.

Too late, we realize I'd turned the sound off while we were sedated and pacified at the spa.

"I know where it is!!" I yell, blood pressure already rising, pupils dilating. "Don't move!"

I jump out of the car and race up the long walkway back into the sweet peaceful spa.

"I need to get back in there," I roar as gently as I can, pointing my finger toward the curtained rooms beyond.

The two tall lithe women behind the desks, the ones who dress in loose black silk and talk only in whispers, just stare at me as if they've never seen me before, then nod their heads. I suppose I look different than even ten minutes earlier, when I'd floated out.

I try to walk, not run, to the locker room, where we'd changed back to our "regular selves" and plopped our spa bathrobes into big wicker baskets.

Gone.

Not one used bathrobe in the room.

An attendant notices my wild eyes and directs me down a hallway to a well-hidden cleaning room. A man and a woman are sorting the bathrobes into huge bins for wash.

"I think I left my cell phone in the pocket of my robe," I explain breathlessly.

The woman laughs (yes, laughs!) while nodding her head toward the pile of many, many thick cream-colored robes. "That will be like finding a needle in a haystack," she says.

"I'll look in every pocket," I exclaim, and the man slowly begins to look himself. As my heart pounds, I ponder: *Have I just wasted an afternoon's worth of de-stressing?*

But before I can even get to one pocket, the woman shouts, "You have good karma!" and yes, in her hand is my lifeline to the world (and all my contacts)—my cell phone.

I take a deep breath and smile as broadly as the California sun.

Aah, a splendid day at the spa.

Family Reunion

I RACE TO THE BAGGAGE AREA FOR THE USUAL "HURRY UP AND WAIT" ROUTINE, but the carousel begins its screeching circular belch of bags almost immediately. My cell phone rings when the "beep, beep, beep" begins and 150 newly-arrived passengers swoop in to retrieve their bags before anyone else.

"Hello," I chirp cheerily on my cell while scanning each bag on the merry-go-round.

"We're here to pick you up," my daughter welcomes me, in a stressed tone with a capital S. "Come out the doors as quickly as you can. Security guys are watching."

"Bag's just about here!" I trill. "Can't wait to see you!"

But she's already shut off her phone.

As the suitcases circle, I wonder about daughter's use of the word "we." Our plan had been for her to leave the two kids at home with her husband so we could have some blessed "just mom/daughter" time before the madhouse of a family reunion. We rarely have time to finish a sentence these days—a one-hour car ride with just the two of us sounded like heaven.

Just as my large once-forest-green, now-cooked-artichoke-brown bag sails by, my cell rings.

I pick up the duffel with a yank as I answer.

"Where are you?" sweet daughter shouts.

"Got it!" I reply.

"We're right at the doors!"

I begin to run to the right side of the baggage area but stop in confusion. A similar set of doors is also located on the left side. And they each display a sign that says, "Pick-Up: Taxi, Bus, Car."

Which doors should I go through?

I stand in the middle of the large noisy room, vacillating. My cell rings again. Damn.

I shove my hand into my cavernous purse, the one that reminds me of Hermione's magic bag in *Harry Potter*, where she pulls out books, clothes, a tent, and a shovel. My fingers search for my phone with no luck. My ring tone blares to the Beatles tune of "HELP!" but I can't find it anywhere.

So, I bend down in the middle of 100 bustling people and pull out my wallet, makeup bag, roll of Mentos, pack of red licorice sticks, favorite pink pen, hairbrush, and then finally, my phone.

A voice mail awaits me: "WHERE ARE YOU?"

I hit Reply back and scream, "Which set of doors?"

Daughter shouts back, "What? THE doors. We're by the red car. Quick!"

I throw everything back into my witching bag and take a wild guess, going for the left-hand-side doors.

But then I remember, she just bought a new car, and I've never seen it. I peer up and down and don't see anyone I recognize. I open the g.d. phone again and, while standing in the middle of the airport car lane yell, "Can you see me? I can't see you!"

"We can see you! A black van just passed us, did you see it?"

At this point I'm hoping to get run over by it. But then I view a brown hybrid five cars ahead, underneath the overhang. Heart pounding I run toward it with my 50-pound duffel bag, my book bag, my witch purse, and my cell phone at my ear.

Eureka ! My daughter is sitting at the driver's side! I open the passenger door and almost sit on my mother, who, along with three-year-old granddaughter and two-year-old grandson, is grimacing at me as if I've been a very bad girl.

"Find a seat in the back," they all yell.

Aah, family reunions!

Ocean People

THE SUN IS HOT, HOTTER THAN IT'S BEEN ALL WEEK. BUT I'VE LAZED AROUND; I've read fun sexy beach books; I've slathered on the lotion and sat like a beached whale; and I've swum with the jellyfish. Finally, I am ready.

"Mom, let's go for a long walk," I suggest. My slim, petite mother looks at me hesitantly.

"What about lunch?" she asks.

I laugh. She's 5'2" and 100 pounds soaking wet, yet she eats like an elephant. Can't take a walk in the early morning unless she's had a banana and two bowls of cereal. Can't walk mid-morning unless she's had a peanut butter sandwich. Can't walk at 1:00 unless she's had two sandwiches, three cookies, an apple, and a tall glass of milk.

"Mom, it's 12:30. We'll walk on the beach to 32nd Street and eat there."

"That's nine blocks," she whines. She's more limber than a football player and has more energy than a ballerina, but she's worried about how long it will take us to reach the snack bar.

"We'll walk fast," I answer, and we smile at each other as we feel the wet sand squoosh between our toes, hear the roar of the waves just feet away, and watch the children scream and race back and forth among the froth.

We are ocean people, my mom and I, and we love our time at the New Jersey beach. We talk little during our fast-paced walk. I think of the gritty sand; the gloriously long, non-rushed day ahead; the hot, hot sun on our backs. She probably thinks about food and how soon we'll be at the 32nd Street snack bar.

Finally, thirty minutes later, the lifeguard stand appears. All we have to do now is walk up the beach to the street and the hamburger stand. I glance at my mom, who's staring at something with a frown on her face. The hot air is waving like a mirage in the desert. The distance to the snack bar looks like a mile. I know in actuality that it's less than a three-minute walk, but I also notice the children and adults hopping up and down as they walk toward the street.

"Carry me?" Mom asks hopefully.

"In your dreams." I laugh and begin to walk fast. Then I run. The sand is hotter than Hades. It's burning my feet. I feel like Lawrence of Arabia, only he wore white robes and thick sandals.

I turn to look for my mom. She's disappeared. Oh My God. Did she get sucked into the burning sand? Where is she? I can't stand and look. I am seriously getting second-degree burns. I run to the hamburger stand and stop on the small wooden boardwalk they have placed for people in dire straits, like me.

"Mom!" I shout over the roar of people and ocean waves. I see a tiny spot, a shadow, move. Then I see her more clearly. She is standing next to a lone trashcan in the middle of the hot sand.

"There's shade here! I'm not moving," she screams at me.

I sigh and run back over the sand to rescue my stranded mother. As I suspect, when she sees me coming toward her, she sucks in a deep breath and races toward me, tears of pain in her eyes. We run together toward the snack bar, and I worry about her lungs and her heart. I'm almost 30 years younger, and I walk every day for sport. Her face is hot and sweaty and squints in discomfort.

Finally, we reach the boardwalk and hobble toward the snack bar.

"I think my feet are burned," she says to me, breathing hard.

"I think mine are, too," I answer. We look at each other and start laughing. Two fools are we. I walk gingerly toward the teenager behind the counter to ask for a bucket of cold water for our feet, but first, I have to stop our giggles.

Ah, how we love the beach.

How Was Your Vacation, Erma?

REMEMBER THOSE FIRST DAYS OF SCHOOL, WHEN THE TEACHER ASKED YOU TO write about your summer vacation? What did you focus on? The days at the pool? The hours riding your bike aimlessly on your neighborhood streets? Maybe your family drove for hours and hours to camp in mosquito-filled woods where the frog hums kept you up every night.

As I thought about my recent summer vacation at the shore, Erma Bombeck came to mind. She was great at finding the humor in the everyday calamities of life. Here's a short synopsis of "what I did on my summer vacation."

- Rolling down the driveway at 4:00 a.m., my daughter drove her old (i.e. messy and quite used) SUV filled with suitcases, cooler, sheets/towels, one ten-year-old boy, and me to "beat the traffic." (Her husband drove the cleaner sedan with their two other children and three other suitcases.)
- B U T, daughter's SUV seemed to have attracted an animal that died during the night in some hidden recess. As soon as we began our journey, our nostrils were accosted with a scent of, well, let's just say "something horribly offensive." For seven hours.
- We were able to keep the windows open for the first three hours of the journey, but as the temps rose to 80 and above, the air conditioning was turned on full blast. For three minutes. Until the smell was so bad we all began gagging. Fan/AC off as the temps rose to

90 and we kept windows wide open on the truck-filled Garden State Parkway. Wheeeeeee.

- Arrived at the New Jersey seashore, a family summer tradition. The condo had a lovely view of the ocean, the kids established whose room was whose, and my granddaughter and I (we shared a small room with twin beds) happily unpacked and then raced to put our feet in the surf. We all fell into bed by 10:00, exhausted from the long ride and body-surfing on the warm Atlantic Ocean waters. Heaven!

- Until a scream interrupted my sweet dreams at 2:00 a.m. Granddaughter (eleven) talks in her sleep! Every night! Loudly! In a foreign language that has never been uttered before on this planet. She happily returns to soundless sleep within five minutes. Me? Not so much.

- The days were warm and sunny and perfect. I walked the beach every morning by 6:15 to watch the sunrise, the shorebirds running back and forth, back and forth, while the seagulls…. Wait. Where were the seagulls, usually more numerous than ocean waves? Aha! A falcon soared along the water's edge, scouting for miscreants. That's when I remembered reading that the town hired an owl/hawk/falcon trainer to scare the gulls away. Mission accomplished, but I kind of missed the call of the gulls.

- Bike rides for miles from our rental to the famous Boardwalk, happily unchanged from my memories as a child and a teenager (where I literally received my first kiss "Under the Boardwalk"). I blithely claimed I could use my granddaughter's bike and she her younger brother's. I promptly fell down on a stone-strewn sidewalk. Brave Madre stopped blood flow with four strong Band-Aids while showing off the value of "no whining."

- Son-in-law cooked some enticing omelets, and wonderful mom-in-law (me) offered to clean up. An hour later, the kitchen sink was so clogged the water wouldn't drain; even the dishwasher flooded. Dirty dishes piled up. Plumber couldn't come for thirty-six hours. More dirty dishes piled up. Could I have rinsed something down the drain that I shouldn't have? I began to blame myself. Plumber finally arrived and groaned, "This is a mess." My guilt increased until he discovered crushed lobster shells piled in the bottom of the pipes. Since we had no lobster or shellfish of any kind, the past renters were deemed the culprits. Phew!
- Granddaughter and I celebrated by sneaking out to the amazing ice cream parlor down the street. We ordered milkshakes that were thicker than sin.

- Vacation resumed, and I kind of wished that summer would never end. *Particularly if I could get a bedroom to myself. And a bike that fits my adult body. And never have to clean up the kitchen. And find a way to drink a milkshake every day and never gain a pound. And if no mice find a way to sneak into the engine wheel.*

Aah. The joys of summer vacations.

A Whale of a Good Time

FRIENDS ASK ME, "WHAT DO YOU DO FOR FUN ON YOUR WINTER VACATION?"

I'm afraid to answer.

Walking. Wandering along cliffs and warm sandy beaches. Watching whales.

To many, these skimpy answers do not constitute F U N.

Yet, when I observe the Pacific Ocean from our balcony, or the bar, or the lounge chair, I can't help but feel the simple joy of walking, wandering, and watching whales cavort, seemingly just hundreds of yards away.

First I view fountains of water spouting out from the ocean up into the air. Some thing, or things, out there are having a whale of a good time.

They prove it by defying gravity and jumping out of the water, their tons of blubber slapping back down with priceless delight. From my vantage point on the beach, I can see the monumental splashes the whales produce.

I swear, they're having fun out there!

The thought reminds me of a scene that happened a decade ago, when our son attended college only twenty miles away, but we rarely saw him unless he needed gas, cash, or homemade cookies.

One Saturday he surprised us when he came home at 8:00 p.m. unannounced, without forewarning. As he entered the living room my man and I guiltily jumped apart.

Yes, he caught us cuddling on the couch, glasses of cabernet half sipped, immersed in the movie we'd rented.

Sonny Boy shook his head in sorrow. "You guys are so boring," he said sadly.

We laughed about it when he left (for a frat party). We thought we were having fun!

I guess it's all in the perspective. I choose to follow the whale's theory: just splash around and enjoy the simple pleasures in life.

Just for fun.

Tunnel Vision

I MAKE IT THROUGH THE SIX-HOUR FLIGHT FROM BOSTON TO LA. I ENDURE the two-hour wait at LAX, a sprawling compound of too many high-stressed, higher ego-ed people, and then the hour hop to SFO.

I hold my breath, remember to release it as we wait, and wait, and wait for our baggage, which finally rolls around the moving horseshoe forty-five minutes after we've landed.

Our driver, as roly-poly as a malted milk ball, leads us to his small sedan. I fall back in the car seat, my guy's briefcase sitting like a rock between us as we speed away from the airport and toward the Golden Gate Bridge, Marin County, and freedom from motion once our front door is reached.

But no, instead the car idles in stop and go, bumper-to-bumper malaise on 19th Avenue. On this beautiful Sunday afternoon, thousands and thousands of Bay Area lovers are traveling—somewhere—but are stuck instead on a concrete highway to nowhere.

I look out the window at tiny duplexes, the commercial shops selling rubber tires and plastic flowers, the newly-sprouted garden lots, and dingy gas stations, and I think … uh-oh.

A hundred yards from the MacArthur Tunnel (the big dark hole we have to drive through to get nearer to the Golden Gate Bridge), I exclaim, loudly yet unintentionally, "Okay, I have to get OUT of here!!"

My guy's startled glance helps me realize that I sound a bit—crazy? —and the eyes of the front-seat malt ball get rounder and bigger as he stares at me through his rearview mirror.

I open my window—car fumes, anyone?—and pray we don't stop inside that tunnel. I could lose it—like an inmate too long in her cell. I could kick open the door and run away from the dark dangerous hole of a tunnel toward—what? Would there be light at the end of my tunnel? Or would there be....

Something is tapping my knee. Softly at first, then more insistently.

I open my eyes (not realizing they had been squeezed tightly shut) and reach for the item my guy is handing me. His cell phone? With a cord attached to it?

Oh, ear plugs.

Wordlessly, he motions for me to put the ear pieces on. I do, reluctantly. What bad news am I going to hear? The traffic report, for God's sake?

But no, I hear flute and cello, violin and piano, harmonizing the sounds of angels singing. The music wafts into my brain and my body and my heart. Sweet soulful sounds symbolizing life on the other side of the highways and small cars and tunnels. Life full of green grass, blue skies, puffy clouds, birds soaring, lovers hugging, children laughing. Joy trumpeting.

The car stops. My guy reaches for his phone and turns off the app for the classical station because....

We

Are

Home.

SEVEN

Relationships

A Perfectly Imperfect Love

I'm in 12th-grade English and the teacher comes up with another ho-hum assignment.

"Write about your grandparents," she demands.

Not so easy. My grandmother died when I was six, and my grandfather went from VA Hospital to nursing home in short order, dying six quick years later. What do I write about? Funny thing is, the one thing I know for sure is that my grandparents loved each other.

How do I know that so certainly, considering how little I knew them?

Physically, they were a mismatch. Boo-Pa was six-foot-two, as straight and solid as a tree, with a large, angular face and thick straight dark blond hair that was snow white by the time I was five.

Nanny was petite, as delicate as a tiny bird, with small wise light blue eyes that crinkled when she smiled; a small, heart-shaped mouth that was always curved upward; and tiny feet and hands.

He was gruff and quiet, with a large presence.

She was dainty and sweet with a kindness that enveloped all who came near.

My other grandmother, Marmu, proclaimed to me years later that Nanny had been a true saint.

"Not saintly, not just a nice person or any of that," Marmu explained earnestly. "But an honest-to-God saint."

How does a saint live with a sinner? How does a sinner live with a saint?

I saw their marriage in stark relief when I was five years old, early one Christmas morning.

They were staying with us and sleeping in my brother's bedroom. Despite my mother's protestations, I tiptoed into their room to wake them up. I wanted to play. Nanny and BooPa were curled up in each other's arms. Boo-Pa was snoring. I giggled, then jumped onto their bed.

They woke with a start, Nanny with a smile on her tiny face, BooPa with a snarl as he jumped out of bed.

He was naked! I'd never seen a naked man, and I was absolutely fascinated.

"Phil," my grandmother admonished. Just that one word, spoken softly but with an edge to it, got him moving faster than I thought a big man should. He jumped into his boxer shorts and turned to look at her abashedly.

"I didn't know she'd wake us up!" he said, ignoring me, wanting only approval from his wife.

She gave him a kiss and told him to get dressed, then allowed me to snuggle in the bed with her.

Lucky BooPa, I thought briefly. But how does Nanny live with such a creature?

Now, looking back, I see it as an age-old question between men and women.

The beauty.

       The beast.

The sweet.

       The sour.

The soft.

       The hard.

And it all churns, somehow, into love.

Unfortunately, I didn't have anything to write for my English class. After all, I never really got to know my grandparents.

We don't love qualities; we love a person; sometimes
by reason of their defects as well as their qualities.
— JACQUES MARITAIN

Love Letters

THE RAIN FELL SOFTLY AS I CURLED UP IN FRONT OF MY BROTHER'S BEDROOM dresser and slowly opened the bottom drawer.

I was alone. My mom was down the street playing bridge with Mrs. Abbot, Mrs. Demmel, and Mrs. Poling. I could hear brother Chuck and his friend Ricky shouting at each other in the backyard as they enacted their own version of cops and robbers. Even at just ten years old, I held onto these rare times of privacy like a drowning girl holding onto a life raft. I couldn't articulate the need for time alone yet, but I certainly could relish it.

My skin prickled with anticipation and satisfaction. I stopped suddenly. A noise—something banging on the floor.

Oh, just the dog scratching an itch.

After opening the drawer as far as I could without its heavy weight falling on my legs, I pushed aside some winter sweaters and crawled my hands into the nest of wool, eyes unseeing, feeling for my secret pleasure. Yes, they were still there!

I had first discovered them a few weeks ago, the old letters, hidden in a place my mom must have believed was safe from prying eyes.

Well, she was wrong.

I chuckled as I slipped out one packet of thin envelopes grouped together with a rubber band. This packet contained letters postmarked August 1944. I opened the first one, an entire unknown world—released.

My dad's love letters to my mother when he was in the war.

"The war" in my childhood household was WWII. My father had been barely eighteen when he was shipped overseas. My mom lived with her parents, commuted to New York City for her job as a secretary, living for the time when she could race back home on the early evening train to see if another letter had arrived.

Most of these letters were from France, some from Germany. They said little about the war or my father's life as a paratrooper, which was the boring stuff in my ten-year-old mind anyway. What I was most interested in, most astonished at, was the way my dad wrote about his love.

He described the times he and my mom kissed on the couch after my grandparents went to bed. About how he longed for her. How he missed her. How he couldn't wait to get home to her. Almost every letter said the same thing. Sometimes he'd mention the atrocious food he and his "buddies" ate from a can. Sometimes he complained that he had KP duty again because he'd come back past the curfew, drunk. Those things surprised me, but I raced right past them, most interested in his romantic words of sexual love and longing.

Later that day, when the whole family sat down for dinner, I'd look across the dining room table at my dad and try to imagine him writing those love letters.

But I never could.

Benji

BENJI HAD BEEN A MERE BABE WHEN WE BROUGHT HIM TO OUR CALIFORNIA home back in the '80s, a vibrant lush green *Ficus benjamina*, about two feet high and one foot wide. Then, for sixteen years he savored his spot in the sunny corner of our dining room.

Until suddenly, we needed to move to the other coast, and Benji wasn't invited. No moving company would guarantee the safety of a splendid, almost five foot by five foot plant.

"I won't go without Benji," I declared.

So we packed him in a wardrobe box for the move, and as we unfurled the plant two weeks later in the sunny spot made just for him in our new, New England home, I heard him sigh, long and happy.

Aah.

He breathed in the oxygen and gave it out, growing in his big corner. The piano sat at one end, solid and staid, while Benji stretched and grew at his end, filling up the large "Great Room" as the Yankees call it.

When guests walked into the spacious room with its high ceilings, tall windows, and a masculine brick fireplace highlighted by built-in bookcases, all they noticed at first was Benji. Not the wood floors or Oriental rug or ivory couches or glass-topped tables.

Just Benji.

For ten more years Benji thrived and, at six feet tall, he owned the room like a king on his throne.

Until it was time for us to move again, and this time, the law dictated that no plant could be transported to the West Coast.

No friends or relatives or even strangers would take Benji—he was too big. But the new owners of our New England home agreed to keep him.

I left instructions: water once a week, not too much and not too little. Let him soak in the light. Talk to him. Enjoy him.

Half a year later, I returned to visit the house in New England, and to see Benji. I peeked into the Great Room, and saw the wood floors and the bookcases and the fireplace, but no Benji.

Ah, there he was, just a ghost of himself, down to three feet by two, wispy, yellow.

Pathetic.

And I cried for our beloved plant.

Who no longer owned the room.

Like a child not well loved, or a pet kept outdoors, or a spouse ignored, Benji gave up. I felt silly, feeling so sad about this dying plant, but really....

Wouldn't you?

[Ficus benjamina, *commonly known as the Weeping Fig, Benjamin's Fig, or the Ficus Tree and often sold in stores as just a "Ficus," is a species of fig tree, native to south and southeast Asia and Australia.*]

Yesterday

My friend admits he's "mildly disabled."

He's a quadriplegic, born with cerebral palsy, unable to steady his eyes enough to read, his arms and chest strapped into an electric wheelchair to help him sit up.

Did I mention he's smarter than a Harvard grad, more intuitive than a psychic, as loyal as your best friend, and wears a smile brighter than a 100-watt bulb?

On a recent visit, I sit on his porch, feeling a fall breeze lightly surround us along with the Beatles music playing in the background.

"Yesterday," Carl says in a fond tone, and I burst out laughing.

Carl and I discovered each other when I was hired to be his Special Ed tutor at the local high school. I was scared to death of teaching such a physically disabled teenager: his speech was affected by his cerebral palsy, so he sounded like a deep Southerner with a dozen marbles in his mouth; he tended to jostle his wheelchair joystick like a teenager's foot on a snappy roadster (watch out for your ankles, I was warned when I signed on); and his body moved spasmodically if he got too excited or aggravated.

Help!

But I had not been told that he could retain information faster than a lightning bolt, and that his sense of hearing put a dog's to shame.

We'd roll down the high school hallway, passing Room 15 on our way to Room 17 for math. Suddenly Carl would state: "What a shame that Mrs. Johnson's husband is in the hospital. At least her daughter is flying home from Ohio to visit."

I'd stop mid-stride in the empty hallway (watching out for my ankles) and ask, "How do you know that?"

"Oh, back in Room 15 just now, Mrs. Johnson is talking about her troubles to Ms. Wanda."

Perhaps Carl was nosy, but he also felt great empathy for the secrets he heard on his hallway forays.

During our three years of working together as tutor/student, we shared a love of Beatles music. So over lunchtime, when I fed him his turkey sandwich and lemonade (did I mention that Carl is unable to feed himself?) we'd listen to "Twist and Shout" and "Here Comes the Sun" while talking about the Red Sox and the weather, *Lord of the Flies,* and why algebra was (not) important.

But then during one lunch, Carl asked me to sing to him. "You know all the words," he said. "Please, please sing "Yesterday" (our favorite Beatles tune)."

If a seventeen-year-old brown-haired, brown-eyed earnest teenager pleaded with you to sing a Beatles tune, could you refuse?

I began as Carl chewed on his turkey and cheese.

Um, did I mention I can't carry a tune?

In Carl's blessed, blasted teenage fashion, he began to chuckle as I sang. I ignored him and continued, "All my troubles seemed so far away...."

Carl's chuckles turned to guffaws.

"Now I need a place to hide away, oh I believe in...."

I learned that day that one should never make a wheel-chaired, disabled young man laugh while he's eating. His giggles became burps which became hiccups which became acute stomach distress.

As I raced for the nurse, I could hear Carl still laughing uproariously in the distance.

He was rushed to the nurse's station.

His mother was called.

His doctor, too.

But you know what?

He never told anyone that his stomach distress was caused by the horrendous singing of his high school tutor.

We've been fast friends ever since.

Carl is now thirty-five years old, still "mildly disabled," and yes, he still asks me to sing "Yesterday" every time I visit.

I won't even hum the song.

The Nest, Emptied

FOR SO LONG, I HAD LISTENED TO THE CLANG OF THE ALARM CLOCKS WAKING up the children, the limping thump of our son walking stiffly to the bathroom, the feminine growls of his older sister as she demanded her time in that same room.

Suddenly, these morning sounds ceased. Daughter was in Florence for her junior year abroad. Son began his first year at a university thousands of miles away, and I was, once again, childless.

The quiet was surprising.

I had forgotten the time, over twenty years ago, when the only sounds were my breathing, my own steps to the refrigerator or radio, my sighs as I thought out loud, the tick-tock of the clock. Once the first child arrived, silence was unimaginable.

I never missed the lack of noise, though. Beauty was the baby's laugh, the toddler's scream of delight, the sick child's feverish moan, the teenager's cry of a friend's abandonment, the whoop of joy when a college invitation arrived.

I loved the excited conversations after school over chocolate chip cookies, and the sleepy sentences exchanged early in the morning in the car on the way to school. Dinnertime was never a quiet affair. As the man-of-the-house expounded on his notion of "charm school" and the merits of not talking with food in your mouth and keeping your elbows off the table, the four of us discussed, loudly at times, the politics of the week, the latest football scores, and why 10th-graders weren't allowed to go to unsupervised parties.

As the two grew, the conversation matured on the topics of sex, the unpredictability of the weather, and Republicans vs. Democrats. The responses were never boring; the walls were never quiet.

But then, a cloud of silence descended upon our household. I could hear myself think again. I heard the wind against the walls, and the old refrigerator's hum of discontent. The leaves of the eucalyptus tree blew loudly outside my bedroom doors, and the foghorns moaned early every morning. The doves cooed outside the bathroom window, and my footsteps marked my every move.

Silence is not golden, nor is it really possible. The absolute quiet was filled with other sounds, but none were as gratifying as the noise that accompanied the happy home when it was filled with a growing family.

So ...

we got a puppy.

The Bed Post

I WAKE UP IN A STRANGE ROOM, SLEEPING IN A STRANGE BED, WATCHING STRANGE shapes shift near me, throwing shadows onto the sheets. I do what any decent, imaginative, middle-aged woman would do—I scream bloody murder.

My man, however, does not understand my night terror. From his perspective, he is awakened suddenly, frighteningly, and unnecessarily by his wife, who has been sleeping in the same bed with the same man for the past, well, many, many years.

But I have been away for almost a week with friends and family on the other coast. So, naturally, on the first night I return, I wake up at 1:14 a.m., screaming my head off.

"Wha's the madder?" my guy asks groggily, sitting up stiffly, as if a five-headed monster is headed our way.

"Where am I?" I ask, breathlessly. I am still sitting bolt upright, mouth open and ready to scream again, staring at the figure looming beside me. "What's that?" I ask with alarm, still not sure where I am.

"The bed post," he answers unhappily. Then he curls back up in bed.

"Where am I?" I ask again, still partly asleep, looking around wildly.

"Where you belong," he says softly, sweetly, as he snores back into his dream.

What's in a Name?

FINALLY MY SON WANTED HIS GRANDMOTHER, MY MOM MARCIA, TO MEET HIS "friend."

"Hey, since Nanny is visiting you, want to bring her to meet Shara and me for dinner?" was how he put it.

Most of us in the family had not yet met Shara, who had been named by us over the past months as "the girlfriend-we-are-not-allowed-to-call-his-girlfriend."

The reasons for the nomenclature were complicated: she didn't want to commit after a previous unsuccessful relationship; he didn't want her to think he wanted to commit; she was worried he didn't want to commit so she was adamant about not committing.

In other words, a typical twenty-something relationship.

Mom, always excited to be with her beloved grandson, was thrilled that she, "the grandmother," would get to meet Shara, "the secret girl-friend."

"It's a sign," my mom sighed dreamily. I just shook my head.

"No," I answered. "Sean sees a chance for a free dinner for him and his date."

We met, tired and a bit out of sorts, at a restaurant halfway between my suburban home and Sean's tiny, hip, city loft. The starless sky wore as blank an expression as the uninterested waitress, who seated the four of us at a table for six.

Within three minutes my mom demanded that we be moved to a smaller booth.

"More cozy," she said. I'd never seen this romantic side of her before.

Sean ordered the Chianti, and Shara sat demurely quiet. I knew she was extremely intelligent, but she looked like Ali McGraw in *Love Story*: long slender black coat covering tight jeans and a soft curvy cashmere pink top; long blonde hair capped with a jaunty flat hat, the kind that only really cute, really slim women can wear. It took her ten minutes and a glass of wine to lose the coat and hat. It took my mom ten more minutes to loosen her up.

"So, Shannon, what do you do?" Marcia asked.

Shara looked up at Sean as if he was to answer, so he did. "She's an investment analyst for a competitor of my company."

Shara jumped in, explaining a bit about her position, but only Sean understood her world of high finances. We Wight women believe in words, not numbers.

Somehow the conversation turned to words, and their importance. My mom told a story about a friend calling her by the wrong name, pronouncing it Marsha instead of Marceea. "Maybe it's spelled the same," she said, sipping her second glass of wine, "but it's totally different. Do I look like a Marsha? No. I'm a Marcie, or a Marcia, never a Marsha."

We ate our pasta, our shrimp, our salads, and drank our Chianti. The conversation relaxed, the laughs got louder, the restaurant suddenly glowed in a golden light, and Marcia continued to try to draw out Sean's girlfriend, er, friend.

"Cher, where does your dad live? Near here?" Mom asked after hearing Shara talk affectionately about her father.

Shara looked at Sean. I think she kicked him under the table. Sean cleared his throat. "Uh, Nanny. Shara's name is Shara. Not Shannon or Cher or Sherry. Shara."

Silence suddenly permeated the table.

Mom looked stupefied. "Oh, well, how do I remember that? Shar? Shar A? I don't know if I'll get it right. Okay if I just remember Char? That sounds close to Cher, so I should be able to do that."

Shara smiled sweetly at my mom. "I don't mind at all … Marsha."

Silence for one sparkling second, and then the table burst into cheers, my mom's the loudest.

A week later Sean called me on the phone for no particular reason, until I asked how his friend, Shara, was.

"Well, uh, it's okay. You can call her my girlfriend," he responded.

I could feel his deep pink blush over the phone lines.

What's in a name? That which we call a rose
By any other name would smell as sweet.

— WILLIAM SHAKESPEARE

Pot Pie

I DON'T LIKE POT PIE. WELL, DEEP INSIDE I DO, SINCE MY BLOOD IS ENGLISH—way back to my great-great grandparents. So sure, I like pot pie the same way I like rose gardens and floral wallpaper and hot tea with milk.

But I used to never eat pot pie because, to be honest, it's fattening; all flour and butter in the crust; butter and flour in the gravy; and then a speck of chicken in there. With maybe a pea or two.

But when I began teaching on Tuesday nights, my guy offered to cook once a week. Hooray! Except my guy doesn't know where we keep the salt and pepper, much less a pan or even a cooking spoon.

However, he serves his Tuesday night masterpiece proudly and joyfully as soon as I return from my writing class, generally around 7:40 p.m.

Have you guessed what his culinary chef-d'oeuvre is yet?

Yes, frozen chicken pot pie.

My guy drives thirty minutes out of his way on Tuesdays to a country farm that sells amazing pot pies. He pops it into the 400-degree oven ninety minutes before I arrive home. He even steams some asparagus to go with the carrots and peas that float in the gravy.

When I race into the house, smelling that delectable gravy and noticing lit candles and a cozy fire warming up the room, I realize something . . . .

I LOVE chicken pot pie.

EIGHT

Musing

Silly Love Songs

Some people wanna fill the world with silly love songs.
And what's wrong with that?
(SILLY LOVE SONGS BY PAUL MCCARTNEY & WINGS)

WAY BACK WHEN, PAUL MCCARTNEY SANG THE QUESTION THAT I WONDER about now. "What's wrong with silly love songs?"

As I write my stories and listen to readers' reactions, I find myself worrying: Do they think this is all so trite? Are my vignettes too "behind rose-tinted glasses" for this edgy time we live in?

A good (male) friend said to me, "A lot of your stories are all about 'female' things." Really? Writing about moms and walks on the beach and sunset evenings with a loved one are "female" things?

Another reader stated that I have the "perfect life." Oh no, that couldn't be further from the truth. But I do like to pay attention to the rainbows in life, as well as the sun peeking from behind the clouds, the laughter emerging from the tears, the rip-roaring guffaw after a friend's comment, the comforting hug of a friend, the deliciousness of a child's embrace, the succulent sensuousness of a kiss from a long-time lover, the overwhelming surprise over the beauty of a baby.

But what's wrong with silly love songs? (Or silly stories about the joys in life?)

I'd like to know, 'cause I plan on writing about them, again and AGAIN.

And, as Paul McCartney sang at the end of his verse:

It isn't silly, no, it isn't silly, love isn't silly at all.

Letter to Myself, 1969

DEAR PAM,

Believe, believe, believe in yourself. Truly, you've got to believe me. (Ha, get it? Believe in yourself/believe in me?). Yes, we're one and the same, only I'm you 50 years later. Strange, huh?

But you believe in strange things, don't you?

Trust me when I tell you, you're beautiful. You're not fat. You're not awkward-looking. And you're not uncoordinated. In a couple of decades, you'll be running ten-mile road races. You'll be stretching into amazing yoga positions and walking an hour a day.

Don't sweat the small stuff. If you wrote a book with that title in your time now, you'd make a fortune! You're probably puzzled about what that expression means, but basically, don't stress about minor issues like whether you'll get an A or B (or C?) in Geometry, or if Dad will let you go out to the movies with Karen and her older boyfriend tonight.

For a teenager, I'll admit you don't worry much except about the large things, like "is something wrong with me because when I look out the window, trees turn gold and white and I feel like I'm flying?" and "am I really an alien who was placed here on Earth to mingle with the creatures from a different planet?"

Keep asking those questions—they'll entertain you throughout your life. But you're so right not to worry about whether that red mini-dress is too short, or if Bev is shunning you because her boyfriend Tim pays attention to you. In fact, Tim will leave Bev for you, but that's another story, and I'm not supposed to tell you your future; I'm just permitted to leave you words of wisdom for that future.

Oh, be nicer to our brother. Chuck is so off your radar now, but pay more attention to him. Decades from now, you two will become good friends, even though you never live near each other, and you'll fly thousands of miles to vacation together, and go to each other's kids' weddings. He's a good guy. Stop treating him like a doormat.

Here's another word of advice that will knock your socks off (and by the way, feel those fluffy thick socks you're wearing now? I'm still wearing the exact same kind of socks while I sit here typing to you, oh-so-many years later). KEEP ON WRITING. Right now (in 1969), yes, I know you have your diary hidden in our underwear drawer, and those two short stories you wrote are stashed between the third and fourth books on the second shelf of our bedroom bookcase. Guess what? In the future, not only will you stop hiding your writing, you'll share your stories—personal pieces as well as your fiction—on a public "web" forum for friends, family, and lots of strangers. Okay, okay, I lost you here, but I'm not lying. You'll also be paid to teach others how to write. Truly!

Finally, your love for our sweet dog Suzie, and her love for you, teaches you to be a good friend, a warm and loving mother, and a faithful companion to several special dogs in your future.

So, after Mom closes the bedroom door, let Suzie hop up and sleep with you.

Love from your future self,
Pam

The Long and Winding Road

As I drive the seven hours to my mom's facility, where she is suffering from end-stage dementia, my heart beats fast and fills up with pale blue, silky pink emotions.

At 6:30 a.m. I've been driving for over an hour. The sun begins its rosy ascent over the paved highway. I'm lulled by the soft snores of my daughter in the passenger seat and my ten-year-old granddaughter in the back seat, covered from chin to toe in a soft flannel blanket.

They've insisted on coming with me on this quick fourteen-hour round-trip weekend to comfort our dying mom/grandmother/great-grandmother. My daughter has always been extremely close to my mom, and she has told herself and her daughter that Nanny is not really there anymore—that Nanny's soul has gone to God, but her body is still hanging on.

Is that true? Is the soul strong enough to escape the body before the body is willing to give up? I talked to a hospice nurse a little while ago asking just this question, and she stared straight into my eyes and said definitively: *We don't know.*

So much we don't know. Sometimes I wonder if my delicate soul could shatter, despite the fact that I feel its superb strength.

But as I drive alone, with two passengers in dreamland, I mouth the words to the songs playing on my daughter's phone. She has "streamed" a Beatles station for me. She doesn't particularly like the Beatles, but she knows how much I do. I realize it's her way to comfort me while she sleeps in this enclosed moving space.

"Yesterday, all my troubles seemed so far away, oh I believe in yester-day," Paul McCartney sings.

But I wonder, is that true? Did my troubles seem far away yesterday but close at hand today? I don't think so. I think our souls are built to withstand troubles, yesterday and today. Troubles interspersed with joy are part of life: the pain and joy of birth, childhood, discovering an iden-tity, finding a career and a meaning for life, building a family, growing into old age, falling into death.

I sing along with the Beatles as the thrumming of tires on pavement harmonizes – "the long and winding road . . .leads me to your door." (*The Long and Winding Road*, Lennon & McCartney)

My mom's door was always open to me, even when I rejoiced in the freedom of being on my own. The first time I returned home from my freshman year of college, a batch of freshly-baked chocolate chip cookies awaited me. The house smelled delicious. But during my childhood, Mom never baked cookies. She didn't like sweets. The cookies didn't please me as much as the effort she made despite hating to bake.

Every time I visited her as an adult, she opened her door as if I were a goddess, a glorious being, capable of filling up a room with light. Our differences were stark: I was the introvert, she the socializer; I liked to curl up in a chair and read, she liked to flirt and play tennis. But we both loved the ocean and spent countless hours on the long winding road to-ward a sunny beach. Before her age restricted her, my mom and I walked for hours along the shore every summer, delighting in the squawk of the seagulls and the suction of the sand.

"All you need is love!" the singing foursome declares now in bright delight.

Exactly. Tears flow down my cheeks as I drive. The early morning sun's glare can be my excuse. My soul may be delicate, but it's not fragile. My soul—all of our souls—are built to withstand the joy of love, and the pain of losing someone we love.

At least, I certainly hope so.

Looking in the Mirror

A pool of thought
stares back at the past in the
shining shimmer of glass.
A mirror of moments reflects that
time exists—physical time—
etching crow's feet, wrinkles in time.

This face is nothing like the one
from thirty years ago—it's wise now,
sad, yet beautifully joyful, delivering
a message of hope—time
wears away the pretty, but adds
the love—

so

much

love.

Acknowledgements

MANY OF MY FAMILY MEMBERS AND FRIENDS MAY BE SURPRISED TO DISCOVER that they're the star in some of my stories. But it should be no surprise that my loved ones are the stars in my life's firmament.

Many thanks to Rhoda Winer, who attended my creative writing classes in the Boston area. A marvelous poet and writer of children's and middle-grade stories, Rhoda was an early admirer of my blog. For years she encouraged me to create a book from my blog posts, and she was my first beta reader for *Flashes of Life*. Although Rhoda is not alive to see the final project, her support is still strong. I feel it.

Kudos to Anneli Purchase, an editor/proofreader extraordinaire. We met through our mutual blogs, and besides writing some fine novels herself, she excels in helping other authors shine their brightest light in their writings.

My publisher, Easty Lambert-Brown of Borgo Publishing, is a creative, intelligent and courageous businesswoman who believes in writers who believe in themselves. Not only has Easty created her own publishing company to encourage independent writers, but she also owns and manages a bookstore, Ernest & Hadley Booksellers, in Tuscaloosa, Alabama.

I thank my fellow bloggers, who have made this book possible. We call each other "friends in the blogosphere," and truly we are, across the world. From the U.S. to the U.K., Canada to Spain, Thailand, Germany, Brazil, India, Vietnam, and dozens more countries, we read each other's blogs and books, comment and review both, encouraging our universal literary talents and gifts.

Last and the opposite of least, thanks to my guy—the North Star in my universe.

About the Author

PAMELA S. WIGHT writes with creative aplomb for children and adults. She is the published author of two books of romantic suspense: *The Right Wrong Man* and *Twin Desires,* and two illustrated children's books: *Birds of Paradise* and *Molly Finds Her Purr.* She now adds flash memoir to her repertoire: *Flashes of Life.* Pam pens a popular weekly blog called Roughwighting (www.roughwighting.net). She teaches Creative Writing classes in the Boston and San Francisco Bay areas (pam.wight@colettawight.net).

CPSIA information can be obtained
at www.ICGtesting.com
Printed in the USA
JSHW020945010521
14205JS00002B/10

9 781734 573053